PAUL

PAUL

APOSTLE AND FELLOW TRAVELER

JERRY L. SUMNEY

🏛) Abingdon Press

Nashville

PAUL:
APOSTLE AND FELLOW TRAVELER

This book is printed on acid-free paper.

Library of Congress Cataloging-in-Publication Data

Sumney, Jerry L.
   Paul : apostle and fellow traveler / Jerry L. Sumney.
      pages cm
   Includes index.
   ISBN 978-1-4267-4197-5 (pbk., adhesive perfect binding : alk. paper)   1. Bible. Epistles of Paul—
Hermeneutics.   2. Bible—Criticism, Interpretation, etc.   I. Title.
   BS2650.52.S86 2014
   227'.06—dc23

                                                                                    2014017410

14 15 16 17 18 19 20 21 22 23—10 9 8 7 6 5 4 3 2 1
MANUFACTURED IN THE UNITED STATES OF AMERICA

For Keith,
a minister Paul would be proud to claim as his child

CONTENTS

PREFACE

A dolf von Harnack famously quipped that the only early Christian Gentile who understood Paul was Marcion, and even he misunderstood him (*History of Dogma* 1:89). Indeed, the difficulties of understanding Paul are legion. This introduction to Paul and his letters has tried to understand him by looking at what each letter shows us about him and combining those glimpses to give us an overall understanding of his thought. This task is complicated by the occasional nature of his letters. Since his letters are writings that address specific situations, he addresses issues without stating clearly what the topic of discussion is and why he approaches it as he does. We cannot even be sure that Paul addressed the issues that were most important to him because he was responding to issues raised in his churches rather than writing on topics of his own choosing. Still, in this book I have tried to hear Paul clearly in his multiple contexts. So the book sets Paul in his Jewish and Gentile contexts, and tries to see where he is intentionally interacting with the dominating Roman Empire. I have also taken into account the occasion of each letter and how Paul responds to it. Attention is also given to the rhetorical and theological argumentation in each letter. Through these means the book tries to set out an understanding of each letter and then more generally things we can discern about Paul's thought.

Beginning with chapter 5, each chapter will focus on particular letters in the Pauline Corpus. These chapters are divided into three parts: Practical Problems and Responses, Watching Paul (or the Author) Work, and What We Learn about Paul (or the Author). In the first part, I set out what issues the letter addresses and the basic practical response Paul gives. In the second part, I examine how Paul goes about responding, what his rhetorical and theological strategies are for convincing his readers to accept his advice. In the third part I draw out what we can learn about Paul's theology. I hope that this structure helps us see how Paul works so that we can better understand why his letters are constructed as they are. In addition, this structure tries to make visible the theological convictions that are important to Paul so that we can understand what his understanding of the faith was. Each chapter also has a Suggested Reading section. The items in the list range from quite accessible works designed for beginning students to rather challenging works that expect readers to know the issues in advance and be able to join the conversation at a higher level. Those seeking further study should also note that the *New Interpreter's Bible* commentaries and the *Abingdon New Testament Commentaries* are available in an online format. For those who do not have access to them through a library, they are currently available on the website MinistryMatters. These two sets will be of significant help as you move from initial study to more detailed work. They will help bridge the distance between those stages of your work.

I thank O. Wesley Allen for reading early drafts of some chapters and offering good advice. I am also grateful to all who have responded to my work and have led me to sharpen my understanding of various aspects of Paul's thought.

Part I

THE ENVIRONMENT OF THE PAULINE CHURCHES

Chapter 1
PAUL AND THE EARLIEST CHURCH

———————⟨Ꮗ◦᠗⟩———————

Paul has always been a controversial figure. He is controversial now because he is often seen as a hard-nosed chauvinist. He seems to have said things that denigrate women or approve of slavery. He has even been used to support anti-Semitism. Some have identified him as the founder of Christianity—and this is not a compliment. They mean that instead of advocating the good and simple ethical teachings of Jesus, Paul turned Jesus into something divine and created the institution of the church, which has been always been controlling and oppressive.

Paul was controversial in his own day for very different reasons. He seemed like a maverick. He was an advocate for what some saw as too easily allowing certain kinds of people into the church. They thought he was harming both the identity and the holiness of the people of God. His manner of ministry was also controversial because he refused financial support from churches and intentionally lowered his social status. Then, he refused to adopt the kinds of behaviors most people expected and wanted in their leaders. Furthermore, he expected those with privilege to accept slaves and women as people of equal status when they were at church. Such behaviors and teachings set him at odds with the culture generally and with some (but not all) people in the church before him.

While Paul was not the only person, nor the first, to advocate these views, he was the focus of much of the debate about them. This was the case in part because he was the most successful church founder of the first century—at least the most successful we know of. He both started more churches and had larger numbers of converts than other missionaries and preachers. Beyond that, he claimed apostolic authority. While other missionaries and teachers pointed to their agreement with the founding apostles of Jerusalem, Paul cited his own experience of the risen Christ as authorization for his own and independent mission and authority. So his churches looked to him as the authority for what was true for the church.

Paul was, however, concerned that his message be consistent with that of the larger church. He often drew on confessions and other formulaic expressions of the faith that were composed and commonly used before he was in the church. He had meetings with the Jerusalem apostles to discuss tensions between their missions. And the purpose of his final trip to Jerusalem was to deliver a gift of money from his churches to the Judean church. He saw this gift as a means of relieving some financial problems and of holding the missions together as a single church.

If we are going to understand Paul, it will help us to think about what the earliest church was like, especially in the time before Paul joined it. The first thing to note is that it was not a monolithic movement. There was difference and diversity in much of its life. Luke's story of the founding of the church has it happen during a pilgrimage feast (Acts 2). Although he has many people remain after the feast, they return home following the martyrdom of Stephen. As they go to their homes, some of them established churches. While the book of Acts tends to make the church agree about as many things as possible and to adhere to the authority of the apostles, such churches were probably somewhat autonomous because of the difficulty involved with regular communication with Jerusalem. This situation certainly led to diversity in thought and practice.

We have clear evidence of significant diversity within the earliest church from our earliest evidence, the Pauline letters themselves. They reveal that there were groups within the church that disagreed about how Gentiles should keep the law, about how ministers should conduct themselves (including whether they should expect pay), about how the Spirit works in people's lives, about how to understand the death of Christ, and many other things. Paul's comments about the church in Antioch (and the place it has in the story of Acts 15) suggest that they held some views that were different from many in Jerusalem, even while they maintained connections with the mother church. Once we get to the Gospels it is clear that various "schools" or related groups of churches have understandings of Christ and his work that were distinct from the ways others formulated their faith. There does not seem to have been a time after the baptism of about the third person into the church when all people in it agreed about everything. Some differences developed because of the backgrounds of various groups, some because of experiences from the surrounding community, and others for reasons we simply do not know.

At the same time, there were core beliefs that everyone within the church held. Some of these were beliefs the church held in common with others within Judaism. They believed people should worship only the God of Israel and that God's will was revealed in scripture, that is, the Torah, the Prophets, and the Writings. (Some New Testament writers also allude to passages from the books that became the Apocrypha.) In distinction from others who worshiped only the God of Israel, the church asserted that Jesus of Nazareth was God's anointed, God's Messiah—and not just *a* messiah who was assigned a task, but *the* messiah of the last days. Translating *messiah* into Greek, the church called Jesus *Christ*. They proclaimed that his ministry, especially his death and resurrection, were the inauguration of the eschatological time. They also interpreted his death and resurrection as acts that established a new covenant between believers and God. Relying on martyr theology, his death was seen as a means of forgiveness of sins and of salvation. From very early times they argued that Christ had been exalted to the highest position in heaven. They expected him to return to earth, bringing God's judgment on wickedness and vindication for the faithful.

Some New Testament interpreters have argued that there were people in the first century who followed the teaching of Jesus but did not hold to these eschatological and soteriological beliefs about Jesus. They simply give no attention to the meaning of Jesus's execution. Such understandings of the early followers of Jesus rest largely on hypothetical reconstructions of Q.[1] But it would not have been possible for adherents of the teaching of Jesus to ignore the manner of his death. Its traumatic effect on his followers demanded an interpretation. It would make little sense to adopt the teachings of a disgraced teacher. At the least, any followers of his teaching had to provide an interpretation of Jesus's death that gave it a meaning other than the usual meaning

---

1. Q is the written collection of the sayings of Jesus that most scholars think Matthew and Luke used when writing their Gospels. Unfortunately, no copies of it are extant.

5

of crucifixion. Any community that called Jesus the messiah after his death would have a great deal of work to do explaining how a person executed as an insurrectionist could be identified as God's messiah or even as a teacher of wisdom. It simply makes no good historical sense to say that followers of Jesus could escape the necessity of formulating a meaning of the death of Jesus.

When Paul became a member of the church, he joined a group that interpreted Christ's death as a death that brings forgiveness of sins and establishes a new covenant. Its members confessed Christ as Messiah and Lord, one exalted to the place of power in the presence of God. So they already saw Christ's death and resurrection as eschatological events. And importantly, some were already admitting Gentiles into their membership. Many of the things that we associate with Paul were, then, already a part of the church's life and teaching before he was a part of the movement. So Paul did not invent these teachings and practices. There were clear contours of the movement before he joined it.

When he was a persecutor of the church, Paul saw it as a group within Judaism that should be subject to the authority of synagogue leaders. And one or more elements of their teaching made them so dangerous that he wanted to see them exterminated. Throughout his career, Paul continued to submit to synagogue punishments for his work. Thus, in some ways he always submitted to their authority and so remained within Judaism in some sense.

Most interpreters who speak of Paul as the founder of Christianity see crucial differences between him and Jesus. While they see Jesus speaking of love and the kingdom of God, they see Paul deifying Jesus and issuing judgmental regulations. This view draws support from the paucity of citations of sayings of Jesus in the Pauline writings, taking that as evidence that Paul is not influenced by the teaching of Jesus. This position is strengthened by the reminder that Paul never met Jesus, and so did not know his teaching firsthand. This understanding of Paul misconstrues both him and Jesus.

To find only acceptance in the message of Jesus, interpreters must ignore a great deal of what we know of Jesus from the Gospels. First, Jesus issues many edicts of condemnation, even as he invites people to repent. We have already seen that Paul was not the first to speak of the exalted Christ who is God's eschatological agent. Rather, those in the earliest church, even some who were with Jesus, seem to have developed this understanding in light of the resurrection. Furthermore, even though they use different language, both Jesus and Paul see an eschatological aspect in the ministry of Jesus. Perhaps most importantly, separating Jesus and Paul so much forgets that Paul is speaking to the church while the historical person Jesus spoke only to fellow Jews. We should not underestimate the difference this context makes both theologically and sociologically. Not only does the church need to interpret Jesus in light of his death and resurrection, but it lives in a very different environment because of the way it interpreted that death and resurrection.

Seeing significant opposition between the teachings of Paul and Jesus also overlooks the ways that the teaching of Jesus seems to shape Paul's teaching. Beyond the few places where Paul does cite the tradition of the sayings of Jesus (e.g., 1 Cor 11:24-25), knowledge of that teaching seems evident in other places. Knowledge of Jesus's teaching is evident in prominent themes such as the love command. Paul does not explicitly cite the saying of Jesus about its importance, but his attention to it owes something to its prominence in the traditions about Jesus's teaching. We might also note that Paul mentions that he had spent two weeks with Peter in Jerusalem (Gal 1:18-19). It seems improbable that some of their conversations did not concern Jesus's teaching.

The church's teaching, including that of Paul, is different from the teaching of Jesus in crucial ways. Perhaps most significantly, the church's message is a message about Christ, about his identity, and what his death and resurrection accomplish. The preaching of Jesus was calling fellow Jews to newly understood faithfulness to the Mosaic covenant. Jesus's preaching said less about his identity than the church's preaching, even if John's characterization of his teaching about himself is more accurate. The church is not a movement that only believes with Jesus; it is a group that believes in Jesus Christ.

Before we turn our attention to understanding the world in which Paul lived, one other issue needs our attention. As we will see in chapter 4, it is hard to know when the church began fully separating itself from the structures of Judaism. Or we might ask when the church stopped thinking of itself as distinct *within* Judaism and started thinking of itself as distinct *from* Judaism. I raise this question here because we need to think about our use of the term *Christianity*. New Testament interpreters have become increasingly uncomfortable using this title as a descriptor for the earliest church. For many, the term calls to mind the structures and doctrinal definitions of the fourth-century church, particularly after its acceptance by Constantine. For others, its use assumes that Christianity and Judaism are identifiable as separate religions, which clearly was not the case in the earliest times.

The term *Christian* (*christianos*, that is, Christ people) does appear three times in the New Testament: Acts 11:26; 26:28; 1 Peter 4:16. In all these places it is hard to tell whether it is a name that the church uses for itself or whether it is a name used by outsiders for the church. That these texts use the term at all may suggest that the church was beginning to accept that name, at least as a designation by outsiders. Paul never uses the term in his letters. He calls the church and its members many things, but does not use the label *Christianity* or *Christians*. Since this language is problematic and since Paul does not use it, I will generally avoid it in this study of Paul.

The remaining chapters of Part 1 of this book will set out the broad context of Paul's life, work, and writing. We will, in essence, paint a portrait of the political, religious, and intellectual world of Paul and the early church. This broad knowledge will provide a context for the more specific elements of that world to which Paul's letters respond and on which they often draw. Part 2 of the book will explore each letter for which there is broad agreement that Paul is truly its author. For each we will consider what problems or issues it addresses, what practical solutions Paul proposes, what theoretical or theological reasons support that advice, and note what we learn about Paul. These studies will allow us to see how Paul was a practical theologian (that is, one who used his theology to guide the specifics of how to live) and an integrative thinker (that is, someone who worked to integrate all aspects of life, thought, and belief).

Part 3 will follow the same structure to examine the letters that bear Paul's name but that many New Testament scholars think were written in Paul's name after his death. When we begin that section we will talk about pseudepigraphic writing in the first century. The book will conclude with observations and reflections about how Paul was both distinctive and how he was a conveyer of traditions that were formulated before he was in the church.

As we proceed with this study, we see that Paul traveled not only with his missionary company but also with his churches. Together they explored new territory. They faced questions and problems that no earlier believers in Christ had faced. As they traveled these roads, they sought ways of being faithful in life and thought. Some of those ways were dead ends or were found to contradict what they believed about God and about their own identity as the people of God. As they reasoned together and took advice from the apostle, they discerned ways of living and thinking that have influenced, even nurtured, generations of subsequent believers. The beliefs and arguments of the apostle have been so powerful that they have also shaped discussions of religion and philosophy among nonbelievers, even to this day.

Suggested Reading

Jouette M. Bassler. *Navigating Paul: An Introduction to Key Theological Concepts*. Louisville: Westminster, 2007.

J. Christiaan Beker. *The Triumph of God: The Essence of Paul's Thought*. Minneapolis: Fortress, 1990.

Michael J. Gorman. *Apostle of the Crucified Lord: A Theological Introduction to Paul and His Letters*. Grand Rapids: Eerdmans, 2004.

Robert P. Seesengood. *Paul: A Brief History*. Oxford: Wiley-Blackwell, 2010.

Magnus Zetterholm. *Approaches to Paul: A Student's Guide to Recent Scholarship*. Minneapolis: Fortress, 2009.

Chapter 2
THE WORLD OF PAUL

--------⟨⟩--------

Historical, Intellectual, and Religious Setting of Paul's Letters

To understand Paul and his letters, we must know something of the world in which he lived. Since Paul wrote to religious communities, we need to know how religions and philosophies functioned and made sense of the world in the first century. Our task is complicated because Paul and some members of his churches were Jews. Judaism was a very distinctive religion. It envisioned its relationship with God differently from other religions and it made kinds of demands that other religions did not usually make. So Paul and other Jewish church members (especially the economically privileged and more educated) participated in two cultural understandings of the cosmos and gods. We must not, however, draw this contrast too starkly. The thought and practice of Judaism was influenced by the dominant culture, as is always the case with minority religious groups. Some Jews (e.g., Philo of Alexandria) used the categories of Greek philosophy to interpret Judaism and present it to others. Others protested against this influence, but even the form of their dissent was shaped by the surrounding culture.

In this chapter we begin with a few general observations about the Greco-Roman world. We will then survey the relevant beliefs of dominant philosophical schools and Judaism to help us see how the church concurred with some viewpoints and set itself apart from others. We will also discuss the ways rhetoricians recommended that speakers convince their audience to prepare us to hear the kinds of arguments Paul makes in his letters. Finally, we will turn to the relationship between politics and religion in the ancient world so we can hear the church's message in the milieu of some counterclaims from perhaps unexpected sources.

The Hellenistic and Roman Eras

The Hellenistic period was a time of scholarly and scientific achievement. Philosophers, scientists (who observed and recorded detailed features of the physical world), and writers thrived. This era produced works and ideas that wielded powerful influences for centuries, and even continue to do so today (e.g., the thought of Aristotle). This era begins with the Battle of Chaeronea at which Philip of Macedon united Greece by defeating the armies of its more southern areas. Philip's son, Alexander, expanded the empire eastward. He created the largest empire the Western world had known. It extended from Greece in the west to the border of India in the east, and from Africa in the south into what we now know as Kazakhstan in the north. One of the things that made his empire significant was his campaign of Hellenization. This drive to make all things Greek was a part of his political strategy designed to hold the empire together by creating a common culture. While the empire held together only a few years, the effects of this policy changed the ancient world permanently.

After the early death of Alexander the Great and the dividing of his empire among leading generals, the campaign of Hellenization continued. Subjects who wanted to be successful and have their children remain among or climb into the aristocracy had to adopt Greek cultural patterns, including learning the Greek language. While there was pressure to adopt Greek ways, there was also room for continuing local traditions. The Hellenizing campaign encouraged creating hybrid elements that melded local beliefs and customs with those of Greece. So gods of Greece were identified with particular local and regional deities. Even statues of the local gods reflected the combining, as they would appear with Greek styles of clothing. This program was so successful that Greek quickly became the *lingua franca*. Greek philosophies also flourished in many regions.

From the side of the Greeks, this sounds like an era of optimism and certainty. From the perspectives of the conquered peoples, however, things probably seemed less rosy. The continual wars that Alexander's successors faced are indicators that the mood of the era was not altogether positive. Still, the world of many residents expanded and the possibilities for mobility, even social mobility, increased. Such rapid cultural changes demanded rethinking a number of common views about the world, its gods, and the nature of humanity.

The Roman era commences with the Battle of Actium, at which Octavian (soon to be Augustus) defeated Marc Antony and gained sole power in the Roman Empire (33 CE). A different overlord now controlled much of the land that had been conquered by Alexander. The Romans brought different ways of governing and other ways of relating to the cultures of those they ruled. While the transition brought some cultural disruption, Rome soon offered official interpretations of its presence and activity that proclaimed that it was ushering in a period of peace and prosperity. Again, the conquered often did not experience the presence of their rulers in just that way. The revolts in Judea demonstrate that such was the case there.

The Roman conquests both displaced masses of people and helped strengthen some elements of Hellenism. Rome collected hundreds of thousands of slaves from among those they defeated. Many of those enslaved were well educated. So Rome brought home physicians, philosophers, and craftspeople who shared their knowledge, taught Roman children, and significantly influenced political and philosophical thought. The multiple ways that the cultural hybridizing had worked in Hellenistic times continued in Roman times with the new partner having a more powerful role. The control of Rome also drew attention to the powerlessness of the individual to determine many things about his or her own life. Thus, it produced an interest in finding ways of being free in the face of power, whether that power was the empire or fate.

Philosophies

In the ancient world, schools of philosophy played roles we commonly assign to religion. It was philosophy that debated matters of ethics rather than religion. It was schools of philosophy that demanded that their adherents change their manner of life to conform to the school's teaching. Philosophies were more concerned about beliefs of adherents than were most cults. In these important ways, Judaism and the church had many of the characteristics normally seen in philosophies.

Middle Platonism

The school of thought associated with the work of Plato is known as the Academy. It went through a number of shifts in thought between Plato (429–347 BCE) and the first century. Under the leadership of Antiochus of Ascalon (130–67 BCE) and his successors, the Academy returned to many elements of Plato's philosophy that had been abandoned. Plato believed that the things we see in the world are defective reflections or shadows of what is truly real and valuable. He argued that the spiritual realm of the "ideas" was the place of full reality, and the world we perceive with our senses is a pale reflection of the ideal forms there. So, for example, every chair is a reflection of the idea of what constitutes a chair in the spiritual realm. You recognize the many forms of chairs as chairs because your soul comes from that highest realm and has seen that ideal. Thus, it remembers that ideal when it sees a chair here.

Plato's famous allegory of the cave (*Republic* 7, 514A-19A) explains what he means. He says that being human is like being born in a cave facing the wall and unable to turn around. Outside the cave a large fire burns and various things pass between the fire and you. Because you can only see the shadow, you mistake it for reality. In this allegory, the things that pass between you and the fire are the things from the realm of "ideas" and the shadows on the cave wall represent the things we see in the world. A few people manage to escape their chains and see the fire. Some even go on outside and see the sun, the real source of light and so the real truth. It is then the duty of those who have seen to return to tell others what they have seen. Most people, however, will not believe what these seers report because it seems too crazy. They prefer the world they know. Those who free themselves from the cave do so by developing their powers of self-knowledge and finally attaining glimpses of true knowledge of the nature of God in a mystical experience.

Plato believed that souls are eternal. They existed before coming into an earthly body and continue to exist after death. This was a relatively rare belief in his time. As we have noted, humans recognize various things in the world (objects like chairs and characteristics such as justice) because their souls have seen them in their real state in the realm of forms. Bodies are temporary vehicles for the soul. The soul's vision is dimmed by its residence in a body. When the soul leaves the body at death, it returns to its true home in the realm of "ideas."

Plato does not think that the source of all that exists is a personal being. The ultimate source of all is the Good, an unchanging principle from which all else flows. All things in the realm of ideas are summed up in this First Principle. It is the absolute being that is worthy of worship, but it does not respond to human interaction because it is not personal and cannot change because it is perfect. Middle Platonists tried to reconcile Plato's First Principle with Aristotle's Unmoved Mover. In doing so, Plato's "ideas" become thoughts in the mind of the Supreme Mind. This ultimate being is absolutely transcendent. Thus, there must be a hierarchy of intermediaries between God and humans.

In addition to the obligation to spread the truth about reality, Plato thought that those with this knowledge should conform their behavior to the nature of God. The goal of ethics, then, is assimilation to God (the First Principle) as far as possible. Philosophers must seek to conduct their lives in accord with the characteristics of God and in accord with the soul's nature.

As we will see in our study of 1 Corinthians, some members of Paul's churches were influenced by ideas found in Platonism. While very few (if any) of those church members would have been students in the Academy, the ideas that filtered out into the broader culture from it seemed compatible with some things they heard from Paul. Paul vehemently rejected some of those inferences, even as he may have been open to others.

Epicureans

Epicurus (341–270 BCE) opened his first school in 311. He soon moved to Athens and opened his house garden as the place to practice his philosophy. Those who joined became a close-knit community that regularly met and lived secluded and austere lives. His community included both women and slaves, a very uncommon feature in the ancient world. In comparison with other schools, Epicureans preserved the philosophy of their founder without mixing it with the doctrines of others.

Epicureans contend that all things in the cosmos are made of matter. The smallest units of matter are atoms, which come in different sizes and shapes. These atoms are governed by laws that direct their movements and determine what combinations come together to form the things that exist. This sounds much like current understandings of the way the physical world works. While we see the world working according to the laws of nature, some people also say there is a part of humans (e.g., souls) or of all that is (e.g., God) that is not material. Epicureans said all things, including the gods and souls, are composed of matter. Epicurus, however, said that atoms on occasion swerve so that they come in contact with other atoms. This gave him a way to allow humans to assert free will.

Epicureans were often accused of being atheists because they said that the gods took no interest in human affairs and that sacrifices did not influence them. But Epicureans did believe the gods exist. They saw gods as beings made of a better type of matter than humans and who live in other realms. Thus, they are superior. Humans can be relieved that gods do not interfere in human affairs, because it means they need not fear the gods. But it also means there is no providence. People should worship and make sacrifices to the gods because they are superior and worthy of honor, but not out of fear or to elicit a favor. In practice, Epicureans seldom participated in public, or any, worship.

The material composition of the soul means that there is nothing to fear about death. As the body dies and its atoms disperse, so also the atoms of the soul disperse. There is no judgment, no punishment for evil done because there is no "you" left after death. Death means the dissolution of your whole being. They also say that the soul did not exist before your present existence. Unlike the Platonists, then, recognizing objects in the world cannot be a remembrance from life in a previous realm. Rather, sense perception is the sole basis for knowledge. You learn what things are from seeing them repeatedly. When you misunderstand it is not because your senses perceived incorrectly but because your mind (also made of matter) interpreted something incorrectly.

Epicureans are known for their ethic of claiming pleasure as the highest good. We misunderstand them, however, if we think they are hedonists. They were not constantly seeking thrills and parties. Rather, when they speak of pleasure they mean the absence of pain and trouble. They seek a peaceful and independent state. They avoided excesses because those led to pain. So they did not overindulge in alcohol because it brings a hangover. They avoided sex because the relationships that come with it involve complications in life. Thus, they withdrew from family life. They also withdrew from public life because of the worries that come from participation in the political process. They sought a life free of all things that disturb a calm and peaceful equilibrium. This is the pleasure they cultivate. Epicureanism was influential in the upper classes (the only people who could withdraw from work) until about the turn of the eras.

Some outsiders identified the church with Epicureans. Both rejected worship of the gods, gathered in tight-knit communities, admitted a wide range of members, and seemed to withdraw from civic life. Of course, their differences in the ways they understand the gods and the meaning of human existence were obvious to members of both groups. Still, the Epicureans were a frame of reference outsiders used to try to understand the early church.

Cynics

Cynics saw themselves as the true successors of Socrates, as the philosophers who went into the streets and engaged all sorts of people in debate about truth. Diogenes of Sinope (400–323 BCE) was their founder. But he did not found a school; rather, he lived in a particular way and drew others to adopt that manner of life. The Cynics devoted themselves wholly to ethics, refusing to develop teachings about other philosophical topics.

Cynics argued that people should live in accord with nature, from which one derived the laws of virtue. They contended that the established laws of society were enemies of the laws of virtue. They divided all behavior into three categories: virtuous, vicious (that is, involving vice), and indifferent. For them, most people mistook behaviors in the indifferent category for things that were virtuous. The conventions of society were among the indifferents, so conformity to them could not bring true happiness. Cynics sought to free themselves from this error by being ascetics. Diogenes went so far as to live in the public park so that he would be free of the demands (including limits on telling the truth to patrons) that possessions would impose on him.

These philosophers stressed that a person should be bound to follow only natural standards of behavior. To teach this lesson, they went out of their way to violate social conventions. They were often unbathed and they urinated and masturbated in public. They were also verbally abusive to those who conformed to normal conventions. They did this, they contended, for pedagogical reasons: to prove that social conventions have nothing to do with virtue. As they sought freedom to live a life of virtue and to speak the truth to all people, they were part of the wider discussion about how philosophers should support themselves. The two dominant options among Cynics were begging and plying a trade. Both of these were considered degrading to the upper classes. But the Cynics argued that they could speak truth to everyone because they did not depend on the support of any person for their livelihood. Diogenes was said to beg from statues so he would be used to being turned down. Thus, he could speak the truth even to those who might not give him money as a result of his telling the truth.

Cynics developed the method of argumentation known as the diatribe. In its first-century form, this style of dialogue included questions from imaginary opponents who would make objections and draw wrong conclusions that the speaker could correct to make his own point. Diatribes often included irony and sarcasm, as well as proverbs and quotations from famous people, among other rhetorical devices. By the first century this was a dominant form of philosophical discussion. Significant elements of it were also adopted by Paul, particularly as he wrote Romans.

Some Cynics were less confrontational and less demonstrative than the "harsh" Cynics described above. These "mild" Cynics held the same views as the more severe, but thought other tactics might bring better results. As surprising as it seems, many people sought out Cynics for counseling and advice. Many Cynics were also involved in volunteer work within their home cities.

Even beyond the contribution of an important form of argumentation, Cynic ideas seem related to a number of issues that arise in Paul's letters. Those issues range from how he makes his living and how that affects his freedom of speech to what it looks like to be a messenger of God. Further, their engagement with all people at least set a precedent through which Paul's proclamation in workshops and public spaces could be understood.

Stoics

The Stoics were founded by Zeno (335–264 BCE), who began teaching in the well-known Painted Stoa of Athens. The name of this school is derived from its home, the Stoa, which was a very public venue. From its beginnings, then, there was a public aspect to this philosophy. Stoics developed out of the Cynics as the Stoics began to hold doctrines beyond the field of ethics.

The Stoics also believed that everything was composed of matter. There were, however, two basic types: coarse matter and fine matter, which was often called breath or spirit (*pneuma*). This latter type of matter infuses everything and is identified as the divine or as providence or even as reason. Since reason infuses all things, the cosmos is rational. This finer matter (*pneuma*) makes up the souls of humans and the heavier matter constitutes their bodies. When humans die, their soul is essentially reabsorbed into the larger soul of the cosmos. The whole cosmos is composed in the same way so that there is a soul of the cosmos. Since this is the case, all things are directed by providence toward the good.

Since reason is an element of all things in the cosmos, the cosmos is rational. Thus, it is understandable if a person can clear the mind of misperception so that it functions properly, in accord with nature. For Stoics, the soul is constituted as reason, and so emotions are an unnatural movement of the soul. Thus, to understand properly, one must get rid of emotions because they are false judgments. Stoics did not withdraw to accomplish this as the Epicureans did; rather, they sought ways to help the soul function properly. The wise can endure difficulties without having their equanimity disturbed because they recognize that the cosmos operates in a rational way. By relying on reason the wise attain a fulfilling life that is not disturbed by emotion; the reasoned life is lived in accord with nature.

The central concern of Stoics, as with Epicureans and Cynics, was ethics. They saw virtue as the goal of life. Virtue was not one characteristic among others; it was a fixed disposition of the soul that was shaped by reason. Stoics argued that virtue was all one needed to obtain the happy life. They maintained the threefold division of types of behavior developed by the Cynics (virtuous, vicious, indifferent). Unlike the Cynics, they said some indifferents are preferred (e.g., wealth is preferred to poverty), but they are not necessary for happiness because they are not necessary for a person to act in accord with nature. Still some behaviors lead to virtue while others point one toward vice. Thus, the wise person will choose the indifferent things that tend toward virtue.

Stoics argued that things people usually value (family, friends, health, social position, and so on) are "indifferents," things that do not alter the wise person's ability to live in accord with reason. Among these indifferents is community. Thus, the wise person does not need a community to obtain happiness.

Virtue, this life according to reason, is not an extraordinary demand because it is not unnatural. After all, the soul is reason. The healthy-minded person will, then, be virtuous. The problem is that most people are sick and need to be cured. The philosopher is to be the physician of the soul, the one who helps others recognize and attain virtue. In a sense, the philosopher is an evangelist who proclaims the good news that virtue, and so happiness, can be attained through clear thinking.

Paul and the early church more broadly used much of the language and logic of Stoicism, particularly its ethics. As we examine Paul's letters we will see places where Stoic thought has informed Paul's reasoning. The church's rejection of the values of the world is also paralleled in Stoic thought. There are, of course, also significant differences. Among the most important of those differences is that Paul believed in a personal God rather than a rational principle that infused the cosmos, and he valued some emotions (e.g., love). Paul also thought that life in a community was an essential element in how believers express their faith and enjoy a good life. Contrary to the Stoics, Paul certainly did not think that believers should rely wholly on themselves to attain the good life.

Neopythagoreans

Pythagoras (570–490 BCE) established a distinctive school of thought that exercised significant influence in many areas. (Yes, this is the author of the Pythagorean theorem.) His teaching on the transmigration of the soul, his inclusion of religious ritual within his system, and his emphasis on rigorous self-discipline were particularly important.

Pythagoras traced all things back to a single primordial Eternity. This being engendered the Monad (the source of unity) and the Indefinite Dyad (the source of plurality). These two combined to create the gods. He saw the numbers evident in the structure of the musical scale as a key to understanding the cosmos. Since there is a sort of mathematical order to the cosmos, he was interested in astrology. Because he identified the stars as gods, he argued that observing their motions could help a person discern their will. This makes the cosmos seem less capricious and more understandable.

Pythagoras saw the soul as eternal. It was drawn toward the divine because the soul was itself a piece of the divine. He thought that if people recognized the eternal nature of the soul, they would be better able to endure the vicissitudes of life because they would know that their soul was destined for life beyond this world. Since souls transmigrate, some people can remember previous lives. Pythagoras was known not only for remembering his previous lives but also for remembering the abode of the dead where the wicked faced brutal tortures.

While Pythagoras had this high view of the soul, he viewed the body as an impediment to true knowledge of the self and so of the divine. It is bodily desire that keeps one from pursuing the life of the intellect, a central aspect of the soul. Thus, the body must be disciplined. Pythagoras lived and encouraged an ascetic life that included abstinence from sex and eating meat, and he opposed wearing wool (because that meant taking the clothes of an animal, a being that also had some divine "ether" in it—though not a full soul because it lacked the power of reason). All parts of life needed careful supervision. Pythagoras's manner of life emphasized asceticism and even daily self-examination. His distrust of bodily existence, and his turn away from this inferior world encouraged an emphasis on mysticism. As in other philosophical schools, some knowledge of the divine was gained through mystical experiences.

Pythagoras also created a community, rather than envisioning the philosopher as a lone seeker of truth. This community had a patron deity, Apollo. This religious aspect, which included offerings (nonanimal, according to some ancient accounts), made this a unique philosophy. Most philosophers denigrated religion or religious services and participated in them only as a part of civic life.

The revival of his philosophy that began in the first century BCE claimed Pythagoras as the source of nearly all important ideas in Greek philosophy. These followers produced several biographies of him that made him a semidivine wonderworker who was an expert on the fate of the soul because of his remembrance of his previous lives. This apocryphal presentation of his life contributed to portrait of an ideal Neo-Pythagorean in the second-century work, the *Life of Apollonius*. Apollonius, like Pythagoras, is depicted as an expert in religious and wonder-working practices and as an ascetic sage. His asceticism included rejecting marriage, meat, wearing wool, and animal sacrifice. A number of interpreters compare this presentation of Apollonius with the Gospels' presentation of the life of Jesus.

There are notable parallels between the church and the Neo-Pythagoreans. Importantly, the Pythagoreans provide a precedent for emphasizing both a manner of life and religion. This was an uncommon pairing in the first century, where religions were little concerned about general ethics. Both the church and the Pythagoreans also placed importance on the community as the place for discovering truth and worshiping. The Neo-Pythagorean low view of the body, however, was at odds with the Jewish roots of the church's understanding of the world as the creation of God. This evaluation of the world was, however, taken up in much Gnostic thought and into later Neo-Platonism.

Summary

Knowing something about these philosophies helps us understand how important elements of the early church's beliefs took shape and how they were heard—and misheard. These sketches of some basic views held among philosophers can prepare us to think about how some views that Paul advocates and some that he opposes drew on ideas already known by some in his churches. This introduction can help set the origins of some concerns and practices in a comprehensible setting. A clear example of Paul participating in a discussion that was current among philosophers is the matter of whether Paul accepts financial support from the Corinthians. Both he and at least some Corinthians are aware of the arguments that were current among philosophers about this practice. In your study of Paul you will find a number of issues that are informed by an awareness of the teachings of these philosophical schools.

Religions

Because of its emphasis on ethics and its expectation that members adopt a particular way of understanding God and God's relationship to the world, the early church would often have been seen as something like a philosophical school. Still, the church attended to many concerns and issues that religions of the first century addressed.

In the wake of Alexander the Great's victories, many aspects of Greek culture were imposed on those he conquered. His campaign of Hellenization included identifying the local gods of various places with Greek gods. For example, the Egyptian sun god Amon-Re, who was the king of the Egyptian gods, was identified with Zeus, ruler of the Greek gods. The Ptolemies (Alexander's successors in Egypt) did not forbid worship of Amon-Re; rather, they encouraged his identification with Zeus by introducing elements of Greek worship into the Egyptian worship of Amon-Re. New renderings of images of Amon-Re began to have features of Greek dress and priests began to address him as Zeus-Amon-Re. The creation of such hybrid cults[1] was a common phenomenon in the areas ruled by Alexander's successors.

These hybrid cults seem to have served many of the religious needs their predecessors had served, until about the turn of the eras. As Rome secured its dominance over the east (Greece, Asia Minor, Palestine), such cults declined in popularity. Of course, these traditional gods (whether combined with a

1. The term *cult* here does not refer to a religious organization with a narrow ideology that ensnares members and will not release them. In religious studies, *cult* usually refers to a system of rituals and ceremonies. For Greek gods, such rituals were concentrated at a temple.

Greek god or not) still served as the gods of cities and regions and as protectors of particular trades, businesses, and natural phenomena (rain, crops, and so on). But for more personal needs, some people began to turn to the cults that were combined with mystery religions.

There is a debate about the function of religion in the Greco-Roman world. A. D. Nock[2] argued that the cults that gained popularity were those that addressed the spiritual needs of the time. He identified these needs as escaping mortality, escaping fate, attaining secret knowledge about the cosmos through communication with higher beings, and attaining a dignified status in the cosmos. Ramsay MacMullen counters this view by arguing that the chief business of religion in this era was to make sick people well. MacMullen's survey of inscriptions from this era indicates that when they speak of salvation they are referring to health concerns, not matters related to the soul or eternal life.[3] Nock and MacMullen draw on different kinds of sources for making their judgments: Nock on literary sources and MacMullen on inscriptions (many of which are addressed to Asclepius, the god of healing). So, rather than choosing an alternative in this matter, it seems best to recognize that religions addressed both of these types of concerns.

This dual understanding appears in the New Testament. The word *saved* (*sōzō*) is regularly used in the Gospels to describe what Jesus does when he heals a sick person. In these passages it is regularly translated "healed." Yet the same authors can use the same verb to speak of spiritual salvation. The early church, including the Pauline churches, experienced both physical healing (healing is among the "spiritual gifts" Paul mentions in 1 Cor 12:9-14) and spiritual salvation through Christ. Paul commonly uses this verb to refer to the spiritual and eschatological gifts people receive in Christ.

The ancient descriptions of what people felt they had gained by being initiated into mystery cults indicate that they address the spiritual needs of the type Nock identifies. Most of what went on in a mystery religion was neither mysterious nor secret. Most of the ceremonies, sacrifices, and sacred dramas at mystery cult temples were open to the public. The stories of the myths of these cults were well-known and singers in the choruses that sang in the dramatic presentations of them were often not members or closely

---

2. *Conversion: The Old and the New in Religion from Alexander the Great to Augustine of Hippo* (Baltimore: Johns Hopkins University Press, 1998 [reprint of 1933 edition]), pp. 100-20.

3. *Paganism in the Roman Empire* (New Haven: Yale University Press, 1981).

associated with that particular god or temple. The only secret part was the initiation into the mystery, something that only a select number of people experienced. Being initiated into a mystery was not like joining a religion, but more like being admitted to a special order. Some people joined numerous mysteries and saw no problem with being associated with multiple gods in this way. What was important in the initiation was the experience of the one initiated. (We will return to this point below.)

One of the oldest mysteries is that of Demeter at Eleusis. Its central temple complex is about twenty miles from Athens. There was an active cult there from the fifth century BCE to the fifth century CE. An indication of how open most of its services were is that they had an assembly room in which the cult drama was enacted that could seat a few thousand people. At its beginning, this cult was primarily about the dying and reviving of vegetation that accompanies the cycle of the seasons.

Its original myth is that Demeter (the mother of grain) had a daughter named Persephone (or Kore). When Persephone refused the advances of Hades (god of the underworld), he eventually kidnaps her and takes her to his realm. When Demeter's worldwide search for Persephone fails, she withdraws to fast in sorrow. The result is that grain no longer grows and so all people are threatened with starvation. Zeus, who knows what has happened, intervenes at this point. He sets up a compromise between Hades and Demeter and forces the release of Persephone. Now Persephone spends two-thirds of the year with her mother and must spend the other third in the underworld with Hades. Of course, the time she spends in Hades is winter when nothing grows because Demeter is again in mourning. When Persephone returns, Demeter is happy and spring begins.

This myth of the cycles of the year and the growing seasons is transformed in the Hellenistic era into a myth that related to the mysteries of life and death—and life after death. Now instead of Demeter overcoming lifeless winter she represents the conquest of death. Still, the rituals seemed to continue to reflect the cult's agricultural beginnings. Thus, representations of wheat (the grain Demeter usually holds in her hand in images) may have played a role even when the meaning had clearly shifted to something more ethereal.

Other important mystery cults included that of Dionysius and Isis and Osiris (Serapis). Their developments in meaning during the Hellenistic Era followed the same broad pattern of moving from explanations of earthly phenomena to myths that interpreted the mysteries of life. The most important aspect of the mysteries for us is the religious experience they gave their initiates.

The first-century rhetorician and politician Cicero was among the many Romans initiated into the mystery of Demeter. Several emperors were also initiated into this mystery at Eleusis. Initiates were prohibited from describing the initiation ceremony, but some do tell of its effects. Cicero says that after his initiation into this cult he had a new foundation for life and that he could then live with joy and die with a better hope (*The Laws* 2.14.36). Apuleius describes the results of being initiated into the Isis cult as being reborn and set on a new course of life as one who had received salvation. The consciousness of a new life was the result of having one's being united with the eternal deity. This contact with the goddess gave protection in this life and in the afterlife (*Metamorphoses*, book 11).

These descriptions indicate that the experience of initiation into a mystery cult included a kind of mystical experience. In these experiences, one's own being (or soul) came into contact with the god or goddess. That contact could impart a measure of life beyond the grave and give assurance that the life gained was worth surviving to enjoy. It seems most likely that these mystical experiences were not just of the quietistic type we are accustomed to envisioning. These mystical experiences most commonly involved ecstatic manifestations of some type. Such manifestations would have included frenetic movement (perhaps sacred dance), being rendered immobile, and glossolalia (speaking in tongue). These were common manifestations in ancient mystical experiences and were seen as evidence of the genuineness of the experience. They were important enough that various practitioners were adept at both having these experiences and inducing them in others. As we have seen from the testimony of Cicero and Apuleius, such experiences were very meaningful for those fortunate enough to have them.

Study of mystery cults is important because it can help us understand what the early church, including the Pauline churches, offered to potential members. When we set Nock's suggestions about spiritual needs of the first century beside the things initiates said about the meanings they assign their experiences in mystery cults, we find many congruencies. The mystical experiences of these initiations gave the inductee a sense of importance as the god touched their lives, they gave hope for an afterlife, and even hope to have the freedom to shape one's own destiny. But these experiences were limited to those who could afford both the associated costs and often the travel to get to a temple. The early church offered many of these same benefits to a wider audience. The church offered a sense of relationship with a god. This provided the convert with a real sense of value. The church also offered its members life after death. Finally, it mediated a mystical experience of a god. The promise of baptism is that the Spirit will dwell in each person. This indwelling Spirit manifested itself in many ways, including in ecstatic experiences.

The parallels in the experiences of the initiates into the mysteries and the initiates into the church indicate that what the church offered met the perceived spiritual needs of the time. There were also, of course, differences between the church and the mysteries. The church demanded worship of a single God, while the mysteries accepted the validity of the worship of many gods. When people joined the church they committed themselves to an exclusive relationship with the one God that other religions did not expect. Further, the church had a significant set of ethical and religious demands, even beyond the worship of only one God. While some mysteries had at least some temporary behavioral expectations, they did not call for the observance of an ethical code the way the church did. In addition, the church had no temple, no holy precinct into which devotees would go to seek the presence of the god. Instead, the church identified any place that believers gathered as a space in which one could experience the immediate presence of God. Despite these differences, however, it is clear that the church offered responses to the same kinds of needs mysteries addressed.

Rhetoric

If we are to understand Paul's letters, we will need to think about the ways he tries to convince his churches to do what he wants them to do. We may be tempted to read these letters as though they are composed according to the rules of strict logic. After all, we expect someone to give a logical case for the position he or she takes. While we say this in our detached moments, being convinced of something often takes much more than logic. We take into account many other things when deciding what to believe or do. Perhaps we think about the character of the persons involved, deciding who to believe or who to trust. Think of the ways people try to get you to give money. The humane society does not simply flash numbers about homeless or abused animals on the screen and then ask for money. They show pictures of innocent and harmless-looking dogs and cats that have terrible wounds. They play sorrowful music in the background and have a sympathetic voice speak of the awful suffering the animals have endured. These sounds and images move you to be indignant, sympathetic, and willing to help. They make you much more willing to give than just relating the statistics. Even though these images and sounds contribute nothing to the logic of the appeal, they are very persuasive.

Appeals to things other than logic are not limited to commercials. If you go to hear a speaker in nearly any setting (lecture, house of religion, political rally), someone will introduce that speaker. Notice that the introduction does not simply tell you the person's name. Introductions may include where the person went to school, what degrees they attained, what positions they have held in certain institutions, what they have accomplished, and what offices they have held. These things do not simply fill up time while the speaker prepares. This information about the person intends to lend credibility to what the speaker says. Even if the speaker's message initially sounds strange, the introduction tries to get you to give the speaker the benefit of the doubt. It intends to lead you to think something like, "Well, I guess he knows what he is talking about. After all, his degree is from a prestigious university." Or perhaps you will think, "I guess she is right because she has an impressive job at that leading-edge company." But knowing the person's previous accomplishments really does nothing to strengthen the logic of the person's case. Still, hearing those kinds of things makes us more inclined to be convinced.

Ancient speakers and writers knew that people were convinced by more than logic. How the hearers or readers feel about a topic or about a person makes a difference in whether they listen. The study of rhetoric pays attention to how to convince people of things. When we use the word *rhetoric* we sometimes mean something that is without substance. That is not how we are using the term here. Rhetoric, rather, refers to the techniques speakers and writers use to communicate persuasively with their audiences. The study of rhetoric was very important in the Greco-Roman world. Everyone who got as far as the end of their studies at the gymnasium was introduced to it and it was a part of the curriculum in various fields (e.g., law and philosophy). All educated people would have had an introduction to rhetoric so that they could participate successfully in civic life, helping to shape policy and decisions of their city.

Ancient rhetoricians recognized three basic types of rhetoric, identifying each with a specific setting. Forensic speeches were given in legal settings.

They argued for the guilt or innocence of a person. Deliberative speeches were delivered in political settings in which decisions about what the city or state should do were being discussed. Finally, epideictic speeches were given on occasions such as funerals or when a living person needed a recommendation. Alternatively, the speaker could use this form to move the audience to have a bad view of the person. In these speeches, the speaker praises a person for possessing particular virtues or blames him or her for having vices. Those who taught rhetoric recommended slightly different forms for each type of speech.

A number of New Testament scholars have expended significant energy identifying each Pauline letter with a particular rhetorical type. They often then argued that a paragraph in a Pauline letter must function in a specific way because that is what the rhetoric teachers said should come next. Most interpreters now recognize that this type of cookie-cutter use of the advice of rhetoricians is unwise for at least two reasons. First, rhetorical handbooks recognize that speakers often mix these types. They do it so often that some handbooks list the "mixed type" as a fourth kind of speech. So they recognize the ways that good speakers use elements of different kinds of speeches to suit the occasion and to convince their audiences.

Second, good speakers are not bound to the exact pattern given in the handbooks. The many examples of extant ancient speeches demonstrate that speakers followed the pattern when they thought it offered the best way to be convincing and altered it when that seemed best. So New Testament interpreters must not use rhetorical criticism to demand that a particular section of a letter must have a certain function because that is the pattern the rhetorical handbooks call for.

Rhetorical criticism does, however, contribute significantly to our understanding of Paul's letters. Among its most important functions is that it helps us understand the structure of Paul's argument; it helps us see why he thought what he wrote would be persuasive. We can compare the ways that he makes his case for thinking or doing something with the ways that others argued for their positions or with what the handbooks of rhetoric recommend. One of the things that this kind of investigation makes clear is that Paul does not always rely only on logic in his appeals to his churches. Paul often uses emotion (pathos) to try to get his readers to see things his way. He also draws on descriptions of character (ethos), calling the readers to agree with him because of the kind of person he is and to reject what others say because of the bad kinds of people they are. Of course, he also uses reason (logos) to make his case.

Logos (reasoning), ethos (character), and pathos (emotion) are the three categories of ways to make arguments that ancient rhetoricians talked about. We are inclined to privilege logic and to question the legitimacy of the other kinds of persuasion. But as the above examples of present-day commercials and introductions of speakers show, the other kinds of argument are ever-present and very effective. Aristotle agreed that logic was the kind of argument that should be most important, but he also realized that pathos was often more effective. So while he wanted a speaker to have an argument that was logical, he knew that pathos and ethos would commonly be more effective in persuading an audience. So if you want to win, you must use these powerful tools.

Paul regularly uses pathos and ethos to persuade his readers to follow his advice. We may be inclined to say that he was being manipulative or coercive when he uses emotion and character to argue for his view. When we think this we need to remember that the people on the other side of the argument were almost certainly also using these techniques. So if he wants to have his view get a hearing, he must use these tools. We also have to remember that humans are not simply thinking machines. Our humanity encompasses more than just logic. So while we are inclined in a scientific cultural setting to admit only logic as legitimate, that way of viewing things cuts off a significant part of what it means to be human. Appeals to emotions and to character can (and often are) abused, but that does not mean they are always illegitimate. As you read Paul's letters you will have to determine whether his uses of these persuasive techniques cross the line so that they become manipulation.

We need to be alert, then, to the differing strategies Paul uses to win his readers to his side. If we come upon a section that does not appear to add logic to an argument, that may well be because it intends to arouse emotion rather than contribute a premise that demands a conclusion. Arguments from emotion and character are not without value. After all, if you want to know something about the history of the United States, you are more likely to get better information from a person with a Ph.D. in American history who has written a book on the topic and teaches about it at a university, than you are if you ask just anyone on the street. So establishing the credentials (an element of character) of a person may well be an important piece of information, even if it does not fit into a syllogism that proves the case. We will pay careful attention to how Paul constructs his arguments and so how he tries to convince his readers. This analysis will appear in the sections called Watching Paul Work.

Suggested Reading

C. K. Barrett. *The New Testament Background: Writings from Ancient Greece and the Roman Empire That Illuminate Christian Origins.* Revised ed. San Francisco: HarperOne, 1995.

Everett Ferguson. *Backgrounds of Early Christianity.* 3rd ed. Grand Rapids: Eerdmans, 2003.

Mark D. Given. *Paul Unbound: Other Perspectives on the Apostle.* Peabody, MA: Hendrickson, 2010.

Helmut Koester. *Introduction to the New Testament.* Vol 1: *History, Culture, and Religion of the Hellenistic Age.* Hermeneia Foundations and Facets. Philadelphia: Fortress, 1982.

Chapter 3

READING PAUL'S LETTERS AS LETTERS

———————

Every literary type requires a particular kind of approach to reading it. We recognize this naturally in much of our reading. We know that we cannot read poetry as we read prose. We know that we cannot read a novel as if it were a history text—and that is the case even if the novel is constructed around specific historical events. We know that we cannot even read all parts of a newspaper in the same way. There are significant differences between reports of the news and the comics or between editorials and advertisements. We have learned to make these distinctions from the time we could first read, so they do not seem complicated or difficult. But this is a sophisticated skill, as is evident when people misunderstand the genre. Jonathan Swift's "Modest Proposal" suggested that the poor eat their children and even talked about recipes for them. Those who misunderstood the genre were horrified. Those who understood that the work was irony saw it as the critique of British social policy that it was. Similarly, people mistook Orson Welles's "The War of the Worlds" for a newscast rather than recognizing it as fiction. As a result they thought the world was being invaded by Martians. If we are to avoid misunderstanding Paul as some misunderstood Swift and Welles, we must understand the genre in which Paul wrote.

All of Paul's extant writings are letters. Knowing that they belong to this genre must condition the way we read them if we hope to understand them well. One of the most distinctive features of letters is that they are personal; they are meant to address specific people at a particular moment. So they are very situation bound. They do not mean to address all people, just those named in the greeting, and they intend to respond to what the writer knows about the immediate circumstances of the recipients.

Think of how difficult it is to understand a letter written to someone you know from a person in her family. There will be references to family matters that you do not understand or stories about relatives that are supposed to be funny but do not seem so to you because you do not know the relative's personality. Or think about overhearing that cellphone conversation in an elevator. The speaker's replies to the person on the other end often make no sense because we do not know the person's relationship to the speaker, the topic, or what information they share that we are unaware of. That difficulty of understanding is compounded when the conversation took place two thousand years ago, in a different country that had different cultural values. We have studied about those values and beliefs in previous chapters so that we will have a better chance of understanding this one side of the conversation. In our discussions of various Pauline letters, we will try to arrive at an understanding of the circumstances Paul addresses to help us fill in the other half of the conversation.

While understanding the historical context of any writing is important, it is even more crucial for letters because they are so personal. Paul's letters are not private in the sense that they are intended for just one person, but neither are they public as some literary letters are. Literary letters are posted for the general public to read. They may be distributed as letters to the editor, in collections that are published as books, or as blogs. Paul's letters are private because they are intended for a very limited audience with which he is acquainted, usually through personal contact. Since they are private, he can assume that his readers know the history of the relationship between them and that they know about the problems and questions he will address. So he does not have to explain the issue under discussion; the readers already know it well. This, of course, leaves later readers (like us) at a disadvantage because we do not have that intimate knowledge of the relevant circumstances.

The degree to which Paul's letters belong in the genre of letter is evident in their form. Ancient letters had a particular form, just as do modern letters. Our letters begin with a greeting that names the recipient. In Greco-Roman letters, the greeting identifies both the sender and the recipient. What is said about each person often defines the relationship between them that the sender wants to emphasize. For example, an emperor might write to a less-than-attentive governor by naming how many peoples he had conquered and how many times he had been acclaimed emperor by the senate, and then simply mention the name and office of the recipient. This would incline the governor to be immediately obedient. In naming the recipient and the sender, the Greco-Roman greeting combines what the letterhead and greeting do in current business letters.

The second element of the form of Greco-Roman letters is a thanksgiving to the gods. People included this element even if they were not particularly religious. It was usually a brief, one sentence thanks and it often involved health. Paul expands this element so that it becomes a section that telegraphs the themes of the letter. So careful attention to it can help readers recognize what Paul thinks his important themes will be. All but one, perhaps two, letters of Paul has a thanksgiving. Galatians, written to a church he is very upset with, lacks this element. After the greeting, Paul launches into his argument. The second possible letter that lacks a thanksgiving is 2 Corinthians 10–13. Most scholars think these chapters constitute a letter that was written at a different time from the other parts of 2 Corinthians. Either this letter originally lacked a thanksgiving or the editor who put it with the preceding material deleted it. Whichever is the case, Paul is following the conventions of letter writing when he includes a thanksgiving in a letter.

The body of the letter follows the thanksgiving. This is where the business of the letter is conducted. Here information is exchanged, requests are made, and instructions are given. The body, then, forms the central part of a letter.

Modern letters have a range of recognizable closing formulas. We may sign off saying, "Sincerely," "Yours truly," "Love," "Peace," "All the best," or many other such stock phrases. In Greco-Roman letters, this space was devoted to trading greetings among fellow acquaintances. They of course had no electronic means (phone, Skype) to contact friends and colleagues who were in a distant location, so mutual friends often included a hello to the letter's recipient. The writer would also ask the recipient to give his greeting to mutual acquaintances in that city. Paul often sends these kinds of greeting in his letters.

Ancient writers also signed their letters. Many ancient letters were actually penned by a secretary. There were even kiosks where people who were not wealthy could go to have a letter written for them. Most people (probably 90 percent) were not able to compose a letter on their own. They needed a literate person to pen the message they dictated. But many were literate enough to sign the letter in their own hand. Paul follows this same pattern. In Romans, the secretary named Tertius sends his own greeting (16:22). We often do not know when Paul takes up the pen to formulate a letter's last words, but we do know in Galatians. At 6:11, Paul says he is writing in his own hand, which is distinctive from the preceding writing. If this is the usual pattern, then he may often compose the last paragraph in his own hand. He was among those literate enough to do so.

It is important to recognize that Paul was writing real letters in a form that makes it clear that they are letters. This genre was a choice. Paul could have written a philosophical discourse, or an apocalypse (like Revelation), or a Gospel, or even a question and answer treatise. But he chose to write letters. All the original recipients knew immediately that they had received a letter. Thus, its content was intended specifically for them. This also means that Paul may give contradictory advice to different churches because of who they are and what they need. So he tells the Corinthians that he would rather starve than take money for his apostolic work from them. But when he writes the Philippians, he thanks them for all the times they have sent him money. Paul is not contradicting himself here, because he refuses money from the Corinthians on the basis of their understanding of what such an exchange means. Paul knows the Philippians have an understanding that differs enough that taking money from them does not threaten his independence to speak the truth to them.

We also know that within the genre of letters there are different types. We distinguish easily the differences in style between friendly letters and business letters or between love letters and debt collection letters. Even stock phrases are associated with certain subgenres of letters (e.g., "Dear Sir or Madam:" as the way to begin a business letter when we do not know the person we are contacting). If the subgenre style is mixed, that can send a strong message. Imagine that a student calls home asking for $400 to buy some new clothes. Three days later, a letter arrives from a parent that begins, "Dear Student: With respect to your request for funding..." That student knows she is in big trouble, all because we know what style is appropriate for the subgenre of a family letter.

Such differences in subgenres of letters were also characteristic of first-century letters. In fact, there were handbooks designed to help students learn how to write certain kinds of letters. As early as Demetrius of Phalerum (between the second century BCE and the first century CE), there are instructions about writing. Cicero, a first-century Roman, also knows of the expectations for certain kinds of letters. Earlier expectations of letter style are also present in the handbook of Libanius, written somewhere between the fourth and sixth century CE. Libanius lists over ninety different ways to begin a letter, with each designating a different type. For example, he says that you should begin a letter of reprimand by saying, "I am amazed that..." (number 64). Galatians, the Pauline letter that lacks a thanksgiving, begins the letter's body with this very phrase. Those familiar with the conventions of letter writing knew they were in trouble—and they were right.

Many who compare Paul's letters to other Greco-Roman letters find that his style lies somewhere between personal letters and official documents. Perhaps this indicates that Paul wants his letters to be heard as letters not only from someone with whom the recipients have a personal relationship but also as someone who is authoritative. In his letters he speaks of the personal ties he has with recipients and he identifies himself as an apostle, and so as an authority. Thus, he expects to be taken seriously because of both their prior relationship and his office.

For current readers who want to understand Paul, including those who want to use what he says to guide their faith and practice, appreciating the epistolary (that is, letter-like) nature of his writings demands that we not read as literalists. We cannot assume that because Paul refuses pay from the Corinthians that he believes it is wrong for people who serve the church to take pay. After all, he accepts it from the Philippians. All of his instructions and all his arguments are conditioned as much by the situation and the people he is addressing as his comments about pay are.

If we want to understand Paul's thought we must remember that he emphasizes particular things in a specific letter because he thinks that is what those recipients need to hear, not because it is the most important element in his theology. Similarly, the instructions he gives about behavior are tailored to those particular people and might well be different if he were writing to a different church because the same behavior can mean different things in different contexts. Recognizing that these writings are letters, then, will help us understand Paul more clearly as we see the ways he uses the beliefs that undergird his instructions to address a specific situation because he thinks they are the most convincing to those readers.

We need to consider another matter in connection with the genre of Paul's writings: his argumentation. We have already discussed Paul's use of rhetoric and its recognized methods. The length of his letters suggests that these are not common types of letters. As we noted, they have built into them elements of rhetoric and argument that are recognizable from recommendations about making speeches. We noted that philosophers and rhetoricians knew well that things other than logic often carried the day. When Paul writes, he intends his letters to be persuasive. So he uses various kinds of methods to convince the readers to accept what he is saying. He uses whichever type of argument he thinks will be most persuasive at that moment with those people. We should not expect that he always presents the fundamental reason that he thinks a particular course of action is right or a specific belief that the readers need to accept. That is, the argument he gives in a letter is the one he thinks will win. It may not represent the real reason that he thinks a belief or practice is correct. So we will have to look beyond a single case and a single argument in a letter to be certain that we understand what Paul thinks about a topic.

We have now surveyed the world in which Paul lived and the form of writing with which he chose to communicate with his churches. Before we turn to look at his letters individually, we need to think about how the church was related to Judaism in the time of Paul. That will help us understand some of the disputes that arise in his letters. Some of these issues continued to be debated at least into the fourth century and some raise them even now.

Suggested Reading

Neil Elliott and Mark Reasoner, eds. *Documents and Images for the Study of Paul.* Minneapolis: Fortress, 2010.

Patrick Gray. *Opening Paul's Letters: A Reader's Guide to Genre and Interpretation.* Grand Rapids: Baker Academic, 2012.

Joseph A. Marchal, ed. *Studying Paul's Letters: Contemporary Perspectives and Methods.* Minneapolis: Fortress, 2012.

Ruth Morello and A. D. Morrison. *Ancient Letters: Classical and Late Antique Epistolography.* Oxford: Oxford University Press, 2007.

Michael Trapp. *Greek and Latin Letters: An Anthology with Translation.* Cambridge Greek and Latin Classics. Cambridge: Cambridge University Press, 2003.

Chapter 4
THE CHURCH AND JUDAISM

As we noted in chapter 2, the imperial might of Rome powerfully shaped the context in which Paul's churches existed. Yet, interpreters since the time of the Reformation have read Paul almost exclusively over against Judaism. They have seen him constructing his theology and forming the church's life and structures by identifying things within Judaism that he thinks need to be opposed or adopted. Interpreters have often characterized first-century Judaism as legalistic or without real feeling of the presence of God. In contrast, Paul proclaims grace and genuine experience of God's presence. This reading of Paul, however, is at best a distortion of both Paul and Judaism.

Our discussion of the relationship between the church and the Judaism of the first century needs to begin with a look at first-century Judaism and the church before Paul joined the movement. First-century Judaism was diverse. There was no one way to be Jewish and no single way that the law was interpreted. There were Pharisees, Sadducees, Essenes, apocalyptic sects of various sorts (e.g., those who wrote and read books such as 1 Enoch and the followers of John the Baptist), Therapeutai, and others. While the groups may have argued among themselves (as did the early church), most people within these groups recognized that those in other groups belonged under the umbrella of Judaism. Writers such as Philo and Josephus talk about these parties as groups that all belong within Judaism.

There were, of course, important foundational beliefs that no observant

Jews doubted. For example, all observant Jews believed they should worship only the God of Israel and all believed that the will of God was revealed in the Torah. But they differed about whether the Prophets were authoritative and about how to read the Torah. Some read it as literalists (Sadducees) and others sought ways to make it relevant in the new times and places that Jews found themselves (Pharisees). The vast majority understood clearly that they were in a covenant relationship with God because God had granted them that status. They did not believe they earned it. Furthermore, while there were exceptions (as there are in Christianity), first-century Jews were not legalists.

Even Jews who agreed about the best strategy for interpreting the law differed about how to interpret individual commands and about how to live in order to obey the command in the present. The Mishnah, a collection of sayings of renowned rabbis, always gives multiple ways that teachers said people should obey specific commands. This impressive book from about 200 CE shows that even within a particular type of Judaism teachers debated the best ways to live for God. We should see Jesus's exchanges with other teachers (i.e., the Pharisees and scribes) in the Gospels as examples of these debates in which different teachers are putting forward competing understandings of how to be faithful to the Torah and so to the will of God.

There were also multiple understandings of a hoped-for messiah. The word *messiah* simply means one who is anointed. In ancient Israel and Judah, kings and high priests were anointed. So the legitimate king was a messiah of sorts. After the exile of Judah, the term took on a future aspect because there was no king in Jerusalem. Some began to assign meanings to *messiah* that included more than human characteristics, with some seeing him as one who brings God's judgment and rule, even identifying him with the "Son of Man" (e.g., *1 En* 46:1; 48:10). But just as there were multiple readings of the Torah, there was no one expectation for what a coming messiah would be. Some thought the messiah would restore the nation (Jer 23:5-6), others that he would reform worship in the temple. Some thought he would be a great warrior, others looked for a king who would reign in peace, relying on God for protection. Some at Qumran may even have envisioned two messiahs, seemingly seeing one as a priest and the other a king.

Under Roman rule, several leaders arose claiming to be God's anointed, the one chosen by God to defeat the Romans and free Palestine of their control. In a meeting of the Jerusalem Council (Sanhedrin) that was considering what to do about Peter and John proclaiming that Jesus was the messiah, Luke has a Pharisee mention examples of people who had claimed to be messiahs. Their claims proved false when the Romans defeated them (Acts 5:35-37). When the church claimed that Jesus was the messiah, it seemed like foolishness. While there were many ways to understand the messiah, all would have agreed that being executed by the Romans disqualified a person. Yet, the church argued that God had vindicated the ministry and death of Jesus by the resurrection. The argument about whether Jesus was the messiah is a conversation that happens wholly within Judaism. One group of observant Jews (church members) was trying to convince other observant Jews that the person Jesus was the messiah and that God had begun the end time with his resurrection. All of this debate makes sense fully within Judaism.

When the church begins, no one thinks it is the establishment of a new religion. It is, rather, a group of Jews who assert that the messiah has come. He was not what anyone expected, but his identity as messiah is secured by the resurrection.

We are not accustomed to seeing the church as a community composed solely of Jews, particularly Jews who continue to observe the law, but that is clearly what our sources show us. Consider Luke's portrait of the Pentecost on which the church began. This telling of the church's birth comes from a time when there are many Gentiles in the church, but it still envisions only Jews as present. After Luke lists off all the places from which people who heard Peter's first sermon have come, Luke says they were "both Jews and proselytes" (Acts 2:10). So while Luke's story pictures an audience that comes from all over the ancient Mediterranean world, everyone there was Jewish or a convert to Judaism. At its beginning, the church was a newly formed group within Judaism. As Paula Fredriksen and Adele Reinhartz comment, "First-century Judaism was first-century Christianity's context and its content, not its contrast; . . . this Judaism was not Christianity's background, but its matrix."[1]

The church's life within Judaism is evident in what we hear of its early activities. In Acts 3, Peter and John go to the temple at the hour of prayer, not to disrupt things but to pray. As it turns out, they heal a man and cause a disturbance. When they are taken before the Sanhedrin, the council whose duties included keeping peace in the temple, an argument ensues about whether Jesus is the messiah. There is no hint that Peter and John are no longer

---

1. Paula Fredriksen and Adele Reinhartz, "Introduction," in *Jesus, Judaism & Christian Anti-Judaism*, ed. P. Fredriksen and A. Reinhartz (Louisville: Westminster John Knox, 2002), 5.

observant Jews. Even the story of appointing "deacons" to fairly distribute aid to widows assumes that all the widows are Jewish. Some are Jews of the Diaspora (Hellenists) and some from Palestine (Hebrews), but all are Jews (Acts 6:1-6). The speech that leads to the first death for being a member of the church also asserts that Jesus is the one spoken of in the Hebrew Bible and that faithful Jews should acknowledge that (Acts 7:1-53, esp. vv. 51-53).

When Luke relates the story of the conversion of the first Gentiles, it is so unexpected that it demands an act of God as dramatic as the founding of the church on Pentecost. The story of Peter preaching to Cornelius and the coming of the Spirit on Gentiles is one of the longest in the book of Acts. And Luke tells it or mentions it multiple times (10:1–11:18 [told two times here]; 15:7-14). Finally, we should note that in Acts 15:5, Luke does not find it odd to identify some members of the church as Pharisees. So you can be both a Pharisee and a member of the church.

Paul's persecution of the church also assumes that it is answerable to authorities within Judaism. Once Paul is a church member, he continues to see himself as a Jew, religiously as well as ethnically. He claims Jews as his own people in Romans (9:1-5), a letter from the end of his missionary career. At a later time, Luke thinks it makes good sense to have Paul participate in temple worship long after he had become a church member (21:23-26). Paul's usual practice when he arrives in a city as a missionary also demonstrates his continuing membership in synagogue life. When he enters a city, the first place he goes to preach is the synagogue. He even submits to punishments meted out by synagogue authorities. Still, there has been a significant shift. His primary religious identity is now that of being one who confesses Christ. But he does not stop being Jewish, he only subordinates that identity and its expectations to the identity and expectations of being a member of the church. But he retains membership within both communities.

One of the most difficult issues the earliest church had to work through was that of the status of Gentiles. Many Jews believed that in the end time, Gentiles could be part of the messianic community. Often, however, they were still Gentiles and not quite the people of God in the same way that Jews were. Of course, Gentiles could convert to Judaism and so become full members of the covenant community. At the church's beginning, it was assumed that all members would be observant Jews. When the first Gentiles were admitted, it caused a stir but their presence did not threaten the community's identity because they were such a small minority of its members. Perhaps they were seen as an anomaly or as a sign that the end was near, or perhaps their numbers were small enough that most church members did not try to devise a consistent theological position regarding their membership.

The question of the Gentiles' status took on urgency when they started to represent a significant percent of members in some congregations. The church in Antioch, for example, seems to have included a significant number of Gentiles members earlier than most churches. Then the mission of Barnabas and Paul (which was sponsored by the Antioch church according to Acts) seems to have established congregations that were predominantly, but not exclusively, Gentile. When the number of Gentiles reached a certain point, the theological questions could be avoided no longer. The central question was, *Who are the people of God?* The traditional answer, which the earliest church had originally incorporated into its theology, was observant Jews, those who live in covenant relationship with God. The church added belief in Christ, but the clear indicator of that covenant relationship was observance of Torah in grateful response to God's grace and love. If that is the proper way to identify God's people, what is the church to make of Gentile members who do not keep all of the Torah in the ways Jews observe it? The success of the Gentile mission forces this question on the church.

Before the time of the church, other Jews had debated what Gentiles needed to do to be included among God's people. Some had said full proselyte conversion was necessary, others called for less adherence to the way of life prescribed for Jews. (See the story in Epistle of Aristeas and Mishnah *t. Sanh.* 13.2.) A number of church members argued that Gentiles must fully become proselytes in order to be full members of the church. This would mean circumcision for the men and for all members the adoption of Sabbath observance and dietary regulations that Jews kept. Other church members rejected this path. They argued that Gentiles were fully members of the church without completing the proselyte process and so without observance of the Torah in the ways that Jews kept it. Their faith in Christ was seen as sufficient to qualify them for full membership within the people of God.

These two ways of thinking about the membership of Gentiles were present in the church before Paul joined. Perhaps one of the reasons he persecuted the church was that he thought that admitting Gentiles without requiring them to become proselytes was dangerous not only for the small movement that the church was but also for the whole of Judaism; he perhaps saw it as something that would lead to the neglect of God's law and so bring harm to God's people.

Some in the church thought that identity within the Mosaic covenant should take precedence over identity in Christ. People in this group admitted Gentiles into the church, but saw them as less than fully members of the people of God unless they became proselytes by having the males submit to ritual circumcision and all begin to observe the Sabbath and food laws. These people acknowledged that the church possessed gifts from God that those outside the church did not have, but contended that full membership in the messianic or eschatological community was contingent on being in the Mosaic covenant and so adopting a fully Jewish identity and observing Torah as Jews observed it.

Paul's letters demonstrate that after he joined the church he argued vigorously that Gentiles must not observe the law in the ways that Jews keep it. He seems convinced that some commands were meant only for Jews and that observance of them made Jews distinctive, but did not give them higher status in the church or a closer relationship with God.

This position complicates the nature of the church's identity. While some Pauline scholars argue that the church of Paul's day remained completely within Judaism and the synagogue, most recognize that Paul's discussions of the relationship between Gentiles and Torah observance reshape the definition and boundaries of the people of God. Paul thinks that the covenant with Israel has continuing validity, but that the eschatological (i.e., end-time) act of God in Christ established a different way of being in relationship with God. He sees the people who confess Christ as the community brought into being by this new act of God. There is overlap between those in the Mosaic covenant and those in the church, but not all people in the church are in the Mosaic covenant and not all in the Mosaic covenant are in the church. Paul argues that the church possesses gifts from God that participants in the Mosaic covenant do not possess (for example, the presence of the Spirit in their lives). While affirming the continuing validity of the Mosaic covenant, Paul calls all people into the new covenant of Christ. Gentiles who do not join the Mosaic covenant by circumcision and Torah observance are fully within this new covenant; so are those in the Mosaic covenant who also confess Christ. Those in the Mosaic covenant who do not confess Christ are not a part of the new covenant and so do not receive the gifts that come through it. Jews who confess Christ continue to participate in synagogue and temple worship and to observe the law as other Jews do, but Gentiles in the church do not keep the law in this way.

This may sound complicated, even confusing. It was also difficult for the church to sort out, but Paul was convinced that an important theological issue was at stake. For him, including Gentiles *as Gentiles* is a sign that God is the God of the whole world, not just of the Jews. Conversely, requiring Gentiles fully to become proselytes signals that God is only the God of the Jews because then God's salvation comes only to Jews and those who take on a Jewish identity. Paul argues that in the church (that is, in the community of the new covenant) Jews must remain Jews and Gentiles must remain Gentiles.

Implementing this resolution of the question about Gentile membership was not simple. For example, this solution means that some people in the church kept the Sabbath and some did not. When the church came together for common meals, some adhered to *kashrut* regulations (i.e., eating only kosher food) and some did not. Such differences caused problems almost immediately. As Paul's discussion of the meals issue in Galatians 2 demonstrates, Paul argues that one's identity as a believer in Christ must take precedence over practices within the Mosaic covenant that would divide the church. So while Paul continues to be an observant Jew in many contexts, his common identity with Gentiles as a believer in Christ means that he will violate the specifics of Torah observance to maintain unity with those who confess Christ. Believing in Christ has become the most important religious identity in Paul's life. Paul thinks that all people in the church must reorder their identities in this way.

The importance of this issue in the first century is evident from the number of times the issue arises in the Pauline letters. It comes up in Romans, Galatians, Philippians, Ephesians, 1 Timothy, and Titus. This matter goes to the heart of the identity of the church and of how the church relates to the earlier revelation of God among the people of Israel. Paul argues for a necessary and broad continuity, even as he finds God acting in new ways. Those new things are always rooted deeply in who God is known to be and how God has been active in the life of Israel and its scriptures. The new never invalidates the former.

The question of the relationship between the church and Judaism in the earliest times and that of Paul's understanding of the issue has continued importance because misunderstandings of Paul have been and continue to be used to support anti-Semitism. As the controversy cooled in the early church and as the percentage of Gentiles became so much greater than that of Jews, it became easy for the Gentile believers to diminish the significance of Torah observance and even to denigrate Christ-believing Jews who were observant. The harsh language Paul used to establish to place of Gentiles was soon used to condemn observant Jews or at least to see them as weaker in the faith. By the middle of the second century, some were questioning whether the church needed the Hebrew Bible at all or if the God of the Hebrew Bible was even the same God Jesus proclaimed. As time passed, interpreters did not balance Paul's dismissive comments about the law, which he made in the heat of an argument, with his calmer descriptions of it and his statements about its continuing validity as revelation of God and of Israel's place as God's elect. Regaining a better sense of Paul's overall view can help readers avoid attributing to Paul the anti-Semitism of later times.

As the church developed within Judaism, its interpretation of Jesus was what distinguished it from other observant Jews. Believing that Jesus had been resurrected gave the church a way to interpret his life and teaching as something other than a failure. The church's belief in the resurrection enabled them to identify Jesus as the messiah who was ushering in the eschatological age. The church also claimed that Jesus, as the now-exalted messiah, brought salvation and was the mediator of the gift of the Spirit. While other Jewish groups had identified various people as a messiah, the claims the church made about Jesus made it difficult for other Jews to accept believers as faithful. When Gentiles became a significant percentage of its members, the church may have been seen as a threat to both the religious identity of synagogue members and the privileges of exemption from some types imperial services (including holding public office and offering incense to the gods of Rome). The latter would particularly be the case if Gentile church members had begun to claim those privileges.

The combination of the claims made about Jesus, the admission of Gentiles without requiring them to become full proselytes, and worries about the loss of important exemptions that allowed Jews to be faithful all seem to have combined to distinguish the church from the synagogue. By the early 60s, Nero could tell the difference between Jews and church members. So while many church members remained observant Jews, the church fairly quickly emerged as a distinct entity. Yet it held to connections with Judaism by retaining the Hebrew Bible (in the form of the Septuagint) as its scripture, worshiping only and being in covenant with the God of Israel, and having many members with dual membership in it and the synagogue.

Suggested Reading

Pamela Eisenbaum. *Paul Was Not a Christian: The Original Message of a Misunderstood Apostles*. New York: HarperOne, 2010.

Matt Jackson-McCabe, editor. *Jewish Christianity Reconsidered: Rethinking Ancient Groups and Texts*. Minneapolis: Fortress Press, 2007.

Francis Watson. *Paul, Judaism, and the Gentiles: A Sociological Approach*. Cambridge: Cambridge University Press, 1986

N. T. Wright. *Paul: In Fresh Perspective*. Minneapolis: Fortress, 2005.

Part II

THE UNDISPUTED LETTERS

Chapter 5
FIRST THESSALONIANS

Interpreting Persecution and Parousia

I
n the following chapters (parts 2 and 3) we will set each letter in the
Pauline corpus in as specific a historical context as possible. We will
identify the letter's occasion, locating this moment of conversation between Paul and the church within the context of their ongoing relationship.
We will also identify the central questions, issues, or problems in the church
that prompted Paul to write the letter. We will see what practical solution(s)
or response(s) he gives the readers, giving attention to the theological bases
he gives for his advice. We will see Paul working as a practical theologian and
community organizer who is providing his churches with instruction that
he understands to be consistent with the beliefs on which their existence is
founded. We will also observe the kinds of arguments Paul uses to persuade
his readers that they should follow his advice.

This work of discovering how Paul decides what to tell his churches depends on knowing what he actually wrote to them. But the form of some
Pauline letters suggests that an early editor may have combined two or more
letters to create what we now see as a single letter. There are also places where
it appears that someone added material. Such additions became part of the
text either when a copyist added them, thinking that a marginal comment
was part of the text or when someone intentionally added material, perhaps
to clarify the original text. Our discussion of the major questions about the

literary integrity of Pauline letters appears in the appendix. Our discussion of each letter will assume the conclusions reached there.

First Thessalonians is probably the earliest extant letter of Paul (and so the earliest extant writing from within the church), written around 50–51. Paul writes it while still on his initial mission trip as an independent missionary. This was his first foray into Europe as a missionary. Paul's earlier work had been supported by the church in Antioch according to Acts. He seems to have served as the junior partner of Barnabas at that time (Acts 11:19-26; 13:1-3; cf. 1 Cor 9:5-6). When he goes to Europe, it is as an independent missionary whose mission is not supported by any church he did not plant. After founding churches in Philippi, he went to Thessalonica (Phil 4:15-16). Paul had been abused at Philippi and perhaps was expelled (1 Thess 2:1-2). While again facing opposition, Paul founds the church(es) at Thessalonica. Since this opposition seems powerful enough to require him to leave Thessalonica before he wanted, a very new church was left to fend for itself. His expulsion was such that Paul did not even leave close associates behind to guide them.

Paul went south through Greece and eventually got to Athens, where he again faced problems. Unable to return and desperate for news about the Thessalonians, he sent Timothy (a junior associate) to check on them. In the meantime, Paul left Athens and set up a mission in Corinth. He writes 1 Thessalonians when Timothy returns with news from Thessalonica (2:17–3:8).

Practical Problems and Reponses

Paul recounts the saga of his travels since leaving them to assure the Thessalonians of his affection for them. He does not want them to interpret his long absence as a sign that he does not care about them. Paul spends a significant amount of this letter assuring the Thessalonians that he loves them, so that their relationship with him will remain strong. In the language of rhetoric, Paul devotes much of the early parts of this letter to establishing the right pathos (emotional disposition) in his readers and to demonstrating his ethos (character).

In addition to renewing and strengthening his relationship with the Thessalonian believers, Paul addresses two main issues: (1) the meaning of persecution and (2) the fate of believers who die before the parousia. His comments about these two related matters dominate the letter. They also take us to central issues in the life of the earliest church.

Early Christ believers often faced what they perceived as persecution. Some of this came from governmental institutions, but much of it was social and economic. Synagogues seem to have punished people like Paul for what they taught about Christ and perhaps for the ways they brought Gentiles into the community of God's people. Paul mentions being the recipient of synagogue punishments in 2 Corinthians 11:23-25, but in the same place lists punishments meted out by local civic officials.

Few believers experienced official civil responses to their faith because they were not central public propagators of the message. Instead, they were the neighborhood pariah. They were suspect because they had suddenly stopped worshiping the gods that protected their city and region. They even stopped honoring the god of their profession. They seemed to be different in other social values as well. So people stopped doing business with them. This was especially problematic when believers were already close to a subsistence living. It sometimes meant real hunger for their families. Family members would also have been ostracized. Associating with people who seemed to care little for the good of their city and flaunted even veneration of the gods of Rome looked dangerous. Even more ominous, the believers met regularly in unauthorized settings and talked about alternative lords and kingdoms.

Early church members experienced this rejection, isolation, and economic deprivation as persecution. Such a turn for the worse needed an explanation if they were to remain within the church. They thought things should be different. They had turned to worship only one God, the God that Paul claimed was more powerful than all other gods. It seemed logical that good things would follow from committing themselves to the most powerful god. But just the opposite had happened; bad things were happening to them. Suffering disadvantage and persecution were usually seen as evidence that people were displeasing the gods. As the Thessalonians suffered, they began to wonder whether they had made a bad decision when they committed themselves to this God or they thought that perhaps they were not doing things correctly and so were incurring God's anger. So in 1 Thessalonians (and in other letters), Paul must interpret the persecution these Christ believers experienced so that it confirms their faith rather than counting against it.

Paul devotes most of the first three chapters of the letter to interpreting persecution. His central point is that their persecution is evidence that they *are* the people of God rather than evidence that they are displeasing God. He supports this counterintuitive assertion in a number of ways. First, he reminds them that "affliction" has been a part of their participation in the church from the beginning. Even the opening thanksgiving mentions when they accepted the gospel it brought suffering (1:6). So the present suffering should be no surprise. Paul also reminds them that this affliction was accompanied by joy that comes from the Spirit. Thus, they have a new and intimate presence of divine power in their lives. This combination of joy and acceptance of suffering for the faith has made them examples of how the experience of God in the church is more powerful than the suffering inflicted by outsiders (1:7-10).

A second tack Paul takes is to remind the Thessalonians that he endures persecution and even takes upon himself more of it than most other believers in his work as a missionary. He is an example of the pattern of life that comes with being a believer. He reminds them that his visit to Thessalonica included suffering, but also the joy that comes from the Spirit. In fact, their affliction with joy follows the pattern set by his experience (1:6).

In 2:1-12, Paul describes his own experience and work among them. Some interpreters have seen this section as evidence that some people have questioned or attacked Paul's apostleship or his love for the Thessalonians. But Paul does not mount a defense of his apostleship or authority. In letters where it is an issue, he confronts the matter more directly. Another indication that his office is not an issue is that he does not introduce himself as an apostle in this letter's greeting. So this long section on Paul's ministry has some other purpose.

Its central function is to present Paul as an example of one whose life follows the same pattern that the Thessalonians are now experiencing. He had endured disgraceful treatment prior to coming to them and he faced great opposition while with them (2:1-2). Beyond the suffering that was forced upon him, he took on additional suffering for their benefit by refusing support from converts and working as an artisan to support himself (2:7, 9). Since they saw this pattern before their conversion, it should be no surprise that suffering is part of a believer's life. (We will discuss another important function of this description of Paul's ministry below.)

Paul's third approach to interpreting persecution is to assure the Thessalonians that their suffering is not punishment from God. Paul asserts that God's people have always faced opposition (2:13-14, [16]). The troubles the Thessalonians bear are like those of the first believers. The original church in Judea experienced persecution at the hands of their neighbors, just as the Thessalonians do now. If verse 15 is a part of the original letter (see appendix), then Paul expands the pattern to include the prophets of Israel who also withstood persecution because of their faith. The pattern seen in Paul and the churches of Judea is that God's people suffer when they are faithful. Thus, the Thessalonians' suffering is not punishment for displeasing God. Paul also reminds them that he told them this would happen from the beginning (3:1-5).

The second prominent issue in Thessalonica, that of the timing of the parousia, was also a difficult one for the earliest church. From its very beginning, the church understood the resurrection of Jesus as the beginning of the resurrection of the dead that comes at the end of this age. Thus, they said that the end times have begun. If they have begun and the first person has been raised from the dead, then the end must be very near. The presence of the Spirit in the church was evidence that God had already begun to dispense the blessings of the end time because God had in this limited way become directly present among God's people.

But years passed and the end did not come. Still, they could not deny their experience of the Spirit, an experience that was a sign that they were living in the "last days." So, they reinterpreted the timetable. They emphasized the suddenness and certainty of the coming judgment and their vindication rather than its imminence. If the resurrection of Jesus and the presence of the Spirit were evidence that the end time had begun, the justice of God (seen in the vindication of the ministry of Jesus at the resurrection) was the assurance that God would make things right by vindicating the faithfulness of believers. But this shift in emphasis took time because the hope and the threat of the end were powerful elements in the early preaching of the church. Furthermore, this shift required nuanced expression of important aspects of the faith.

Apparently Paul's initial preaching emphasized the imminence of the end because the Thessalonians did not think anyone in their church would die before the return of Christ. They looked forward to the blessings of that return as a vindication of their decision to worship only God and as a reward for their willingness to endure persecution for that belief. But they were afraid that some people in their church were going to miss those experiences because they had died.

Like many in the ancient world, these Thessalonians did not think that humans were by nature immortal. They seemed to believe that the dead were simply dead with no hope of an afterlife. Thus, they worried that members of their church who died before the return of Christ had missed the blessings that come at the parousia. This may have led some to rethink their allegiance to the church. Why endure persecution if you are just going to die and never experience life with God? In the face of this question, Paul assures the readers that the dead will share in the afterlife with Christ.

Paul devotes 4:13–5:11 to the question of the participation of the dead in the parousia. He first asserts that their belief in the resurrection of Christ should alleviate any doubt about whether believers who have died can be raised to receive the blessings of the last day (4:13-14). He then describes the parousia in a way that has the dead being raised at its inception and being taken up to join Christ before the living. He uses traditional apocalyptic language to describe the scene and constructs it so that those who have died and those alive at its occurrence will be together with Christ.

Paul addresses the timing of the parousia in 5:1-11, stressing that its timing is really unimportant. Still, they must always be ready for it. In this earliest of the church's writings, the shift from highlighting the imminence of the Second Coming to an emphasis on its suddenness and certainty is already evident. The day will come as "a thief in the night" (5:2). The delay, he asserts, should not put the parousia's certainty in doubt. It will be the moment of judgment for outsiders and of salvation for believers. Paul explicitly includes the believers who had died among those who receive salvation, saying that Christ died so that the living and the dead could live with him (5:9-10).

Watching Paul Work

We have seen what Paul's responses are; now we will look at some of the main ways he supports them. He uses a number of different means to persuade the Thessalonians that his understandings provide the appropriate responses to their concerns. He often uses theological affirmations as a starting point.

Paul regularly builds his responses on things the readers already believe. The Thessalonians believe firmly in the resurrection of Christ, so he draws implications from it to support his understanding of the Second Coming. He does this explicitly in 4:14. The basic premise is that Christ died and was raised. Since Christ's resurrection proves God can raise the dead, God can (and will) raise the Thessalonians who have died. Here Paul makes a logical argument based on a premise he and the readers believe is certain. Once this central point is established, he can discuss whether the dead's participation in the parousia is disadvantaged in comparison with those who are alive at its occurrence.

Paul's assurance that their suffering is not punishment rejects one interpretation of suffering, but does not directly explain why God's people are persecuted. His explanation is indirect and rests on his eschatological interpretation of the state of the world. While a misunderstanding of one aspect of eschatology is a major issue, Paul assumes that the Thessalonians retain the apocalyptic mind-set that undergirds his interpretation of the world. This outlook sees the political, social, and economic structures of the world to be controlled by evil. The demonic forces control these structures and work through the people who are in power. When those forces see believers reject the values that support these systems, they attack them as a means of remaining in control. The people in power remain committed to the dominant ways of viewing the cosmos and of constructing meaning in life. To maintain control, they inflict suffering to demand conformity. The Thessalonians suffer, then, because by believing in Christ they have set themselves against those who live by the standards that govern the world's structures. They are a threat to the dominant powers and structures. So certain is this response that Paul can say that believers are destined for affliction (3:3).

Paul does not explicitly set out this construct of reality in 1 Thessalonians, but a number of his comments reflect it. In the thanksgiving he speaks of the Thessalonians turning from the worship of other gods to await "the coming wrath" and their rescue from it in Christ (1:9-10). Paul's description of his life among them mentions their being called into God's kingdom and glory. More explicitly, Paul says that Satan works to cause him distress and keep him from strengthening the Thessalonians' faith (2:18). So Satan works against the good of God's people. Indeed, "the tempter" tries to destroy their faith through the afflictions that accompany faith (3:4-5). In the middle of these statements about the work of Satan, Paul again mentions the parousia as the time when he will have joy and glory because the Thessalonians will be with him in glory (2:19-20).

Belief in a Second Coming of Christ that brings cosmic judgment and salvation is foundational for this letter. Paul draws on it often to support both general and specific instructions, implying that retaining the proper beliefs and behaviors is required to receive salvation. This threat is direct in 4:6-7 and 5:6-10, and is implied in 2:12; 3:5, 13; and perhaps in 1:10. Thus, the Thessalonians' belief in a future judgment plays a significant role in supporting Paul's instructions to them.

Rather than constructing an argument on logic, Paul sometimes simply elaborates a belief they accept. In 5:1-2, he says they already know that the "day of the Lord will come like a thief in the night." Paul increases their attachment to this belief by identifying them as the people who will participate in the day's salvation while others, perhaps especially those who persecute them, will experience condemnation. He again attaches the salvation of the living and the dead to Christ's death, but this time without walking them through the logic that connects them. The strategy of asserting that what they already believe actually implies the point he is making allows him to present a convincing argument that does not require them to feel as though they are accepting new, and perhaps difficult, ideas.

Paul also relies on other authorities to support his positions. He bases his contention that the dead will not be disadvantaged on a "word of the Lord" (4:15). This probably refers to a message from the risen Christ rather than from the earthly Jesus. The early church believed that Christ spoke to and through apostles and prophets. Paul does not specify who the recipient was, but identifying the saying as one from Christ carries significant weight. Similarly, when he gives instructions about proper behavior, he reminds them that his teaching came "through the Lord Jesus" (4:2). Ignoring these instructions, then, amounts to ignoring God (4:8). This authority carries such weight that it comes with a warning that those who violate it will face God's punishment (4:6). This passage combines reliance on an authority with their belief in coming judgment to provide a powerful warrant for its instructions.

Paul's discussion of his work in 2:1-12 employs a different persuasive method. It is an exercise in establishing his character (ethos) as the one who will tell them the truth. He presents himself as someone who not only suffers for the faith, but *also for them* (2:2). Rhetoricians advised speakers to demonstrate that they care about the welfare of the people they are addressing. When people believe this, they much more readily accept your advice. Adopting this way of proceeding, Paul says that he gave them not only the gospel but his very self because he loves them so much (2:8). That love was shown in his willingness to work as an artisan while bringing the gospel to them. He presents working as an artisan as a sacrifice because wealthier people saw manual labor as demeaning. That Paul was willing to lower himself in this way demonstrates his love for them.

He also uses some striking metaphors to establish his ethos. He says his conduct among them was as gentle as a wet nurse taking care of her own children. Wealthy women of the first century often had other women nurse their babies. Paul compares himself to such a woman, one who would be all the more gentle as she nurses her own children. A few lines later he says his behavior was like a father encouraging and comforting his own children. He thus describes his relationship with them in the most loving of ways. If they accept this interpretation of his work among them, they will believe he has their best interest at heart.

Paul's explanation for his prolonged absence also contributes to constructing the image of one who loves his readers. He describes his experience of this absence as being "orphaned" from them and having a great desire to see them (2:17). It took the doing of Satan to keep him away! They are his glory and joy and what he boasts of (2:18-20). He loves them so much he was willing to experience more loneliness to get word about them and to support their well-being (3:1-5). The good news he gets allows him to continue to live and thank God. Still he constantly prays to get to visit them (3:6-10). If he cares all this much for them, he certainly will not lead them astray.

Paul also works to increase the Thessalonians' investment in retaining the faith. He says their initial acceptance of the gospel is known as exemplary throughout northern and central Greece (1:6-10). So they are not just imitators of Paul, but examples of what everyone should be. To turn back would make them seem fickle, and the honor they now possess would vanish.

Paul's praise of them in 5:4-9 also increases their investment in retaining their faith. Here they are the people of light who are not caught up in vice. Thus, they will not experience condemnation. In 4:5, he similarly distinguishes them from the "Gentiles who do not know God" (4:5) and so are destined for condemnation because of their immoral behavior. Such stark contrasts between insiders and outsiders help maintain the readers' desire to remain insiders.

Paul's strategies for persuading these readers to follow his advice include relying on outside authorities, logic, emotional appeals, drawing implications from firmly held beliefs, and his relationship with the readers. The central theological bases for his responses to the Thessalonians' questions involve the meaning of the resurrection of Christ and belief in the parousia, with the accompanying eschatological interpretation of the world that it implies. He uses these core beliefs to interpret the persecution they suffer and to assure them about the fate of the dead and the certainty of life with God for the faithful.

What We Learn about Paul

We cannot assume that what Paul emphasizes in a particular letter is centrally important for his thought, because each letter responds to issues that the situation presents. Still, his argument may demonstrate that some things are important in his theology.

Paul's reliance on an apocalyptic interpretation of reality suggests that this eschatological outlook is a central element in his theology. This viewpoint remains a constant in all of his letters. It is the lens through which he interprets all of reality. Both his present interpretation of the experience of believers and his future hope is inexorably linked to his eschatological viewpoint. It explains the persecution that believers suffer and offers the hope of a future with God. The inclusion of judgment in the apocalyptic scenario both promises vindication and demands attention to ethical living. This apocalyptic perspective is a necessary presupposition of Paul's theological reasoning; his theology and work of applying his beliefs to new situations (i.e., his theologizing) is thoroughly eschatological.

This eschatological theology grows out of Paul's understanding of the death and resurrection of Christ. Paul interprets the two-part event of Jesus's death and resurrection as the act that inaugurates the end times because the resurrection of the dead is an end-time event. Jesus's resurrection is the beginning of the resurrection of the dead and thus the beginning of the end. It demonstrates the power of God over death and over the powers that confine all people to death. Furthermore, it vindicates the ministry of Jesus. By extension, it validates the identity of those who endure persecution for the gospel; it demonstrates that they are the people of God who will be vindicated when the resurrection resumes at the return of Christ.

Suggested Reading

Victor Paul Furnish. *1 & 2 Thessalonians*. Abingdon New Testament Commentary. Nashville: Abingdon, 2007.

Beverley Roberts Gaventa. *First and Second Thessalonians*. Interpretation. Louisville: Westminster, 2012.

Abraham J. Malherbe. *The Letters to the Thessalonians: A New Translation with Introduction and Commentary*. Anchor Bible. New York: Doubleday, 2000.

————. *Paul and the Philosophers: The Philosophic Tradition of Pastoral Care.* Eugene, OR: Wipf & Stock, 2011 (reprint of 1987 edition, Fortress Press).

Earl J. Richard. *First and Second Thessalonians.* Sacra Pagina. Wilmington: Michael Glazier, 2007.

Chapter 6
FIRST CORINTHIANS

Redefining Spirituality

Paul founded the church in Corinth a few months after he left Thessalonica, while still on his initial trip to Greece as an apostle. He went to Corinth after spending some time in Athens (1 Thess 3:1-2). Acts has this stay in Corinth last eighteen months. While interpreters disagree about how the sequence of Paul's multiple visits to Corinth relate to the writing of the letters, they all agree that at some point he was put on trial before Gallio in 51 or 52 (even though this incident is mentioned only in Acts 18). The case was immediately dismissed, but the episode indicates that he remained active within the Jewish community as he was establishing or strengthening the church.

Paul gets information about the church at Corinth from three sources: members of the household of Chloe (1:11), a group from Corinth consisting of Stephanus, Fortunatus, and Achaicus (16:17-18), and a letter from the church (7:1). These multiple sources of information and the mention of a previous letter (5:9) have led some to argue that 1 Corinthians is composed of parts of three or five letters. The large majority of interpreters, however, see it as a single letter that may have at least one substantive interpolation (14:33b-36).

This letter exhibits less concern than 1 Thessalonians with how the church relates to the outside world and more concern with the inner life of the church. The problems at Corinth involve allowing the values of the empire and the broader culture to shape the church's self-understanding and its ideas about how its members relate to one another. First Corinthians offers us an intriguing window into the life of the early church as its recipients struggle to understand how to embody their new faith.

Practical Problems and Responses

The problems this letter addresses seem to have grown from within the church rather than being caused by rival teachers who oppose Paul or his understanding of the faith. The church has become factious. This factionalism is a central issue that influences everything Paul addresses in the letter. First, members are arguing about who their leaders should be and what characteristics leaders should possess. Paul caricatures their bickering by saying that each person says, "I belong to Paul," or "I belong to Apollos," or "I belong to Cephas," or "I belong to Christ" (1:12). It seems unlikely that any of these leaders were involved in the disputes or lent their names to them. In fact, their names probably serve as substitutes for the actual local leaders that the arguments are really about. This is clear in the case of Apollos. Paul indicates that he is on good terms with Apollos, by saying he has applied an example to himself and Apollos so they will get the point (4:6) and by mentioning that Apollos is with him as he writes (16:12).

The dominant theological issue involves Christian spirituality. Many in Corinth think that the Spirit makes people powerful and impressive. This understanding of the result of coming into contact with a god was common in religions of the Greco-Roman world. The Corinthians have simply transferred into the church the understanding of spirituality found in the religions around them. The Corinthians disagree among themselves about which things are the most impressive, but all agree that those who are impressive and powerful possess a greater share of the Spirit and so should be leaders.

Paul devotes all of chapters 1–4 to leadership and the factions that are growing around selected leaders. This matter involves how believers understand God, how God is revealed in Christ, and how the community should be structured. The core of his response to their divisiveness is 1:18–2:16. In this section Paul argues that believers must adopt a radically different way of perceiving all things. He opposes the wisdom of God to the "wisdom of this age" (2:6). The central lens for seeing things in this new way is the message (or word) of the cross (1:18). Believers must reinterpret all of reality through the cross. The cross reveals how to understand God, life within the church, and even the future. Christ's death for others in accord with the will of God reveals the way believers should interpret the world and construct their lives, including their communal lives in the church.

This is a radical assertion. This self-disclosure of God on the cross puts all other wisdom under God's judgment as it establishes a new norm for life. It sounds very foolish to proclaim that the best place to see who God is and what God wants is in the execution of a convicted insurrectionist (Jesus). It is the equivalent of saying that the best place to see God is in the torture of a terrorist. This made no more sense in their world than it does in ours. That is why Paul says it is foolishness to everyone who has not experienced the salvation that comes through Christ. Not even the powers that control the political, social, and economic structures of the world could figure it out. If they had known, Paul says, they would not have crucified Jesus because that becomes the act that signals the beginning of their defeat (2:8).

Of course, the "word of the cross" is complete only if it includes the resurrection as the vindication of the way of life that led to Jesus's death. Perhaps that makes things all the more strange, though, because the resurrection declares that the self-giving death of Jesus is the pattern of existence God approves. When the powers thought they were defeating Jesus and God's purposes, they actually cleared the way for the power and will of God to be seen in the resurrection's vindication of the cross.

The cross, then, sets the pattern for seeing the truth about the world and for determining how to live in relation to one another, including how leaders should function. Rather than evaluating teachers by whether they are impressive, believers should assess leaders by whether they put the good of others before their own good as Christ did on the cross. Paul reminds them that his conduct in relation to them followed this pattern; he lowered himself and put their good ahead of his own (2:1-4). The result was that they came to know God and to receive the gifts of salvation. Now they must evaluate their leaders and relations with one another through the lens of the "word of the cross." Paul believes that adopting this perspective will put an end to their internal strife and their competition about leaders.

Beyond troubles related to identifying with leaders, Paul's various sources of information have told him of several other problems. Some members are suing each other and perhaps are cheating each other in business deals

(6:1-11). Some have misunderstood the implications of their faith for sexual ethics. On the one hand, a man is having an affair with his stepmother (who may well have been closer to his age than to that of his father). Some members of the church are proud of this exhibition of freedom (5:1-13). It is probably also this group that thinks it is appropriate for believers to employ the services of prostitutes (6:12-20). On the other hand, there are members who seem to think that sex even within marriage is wrong (7:1-40). This is the first issue Paul responds to from their letter. The issues concerning sexual ethics seem to stem from viewing the body as unimportant and perhaps thinking it is unable to affect the soul. They may also have misunderstood Paul's assertion that justification is by faith without "the works of the law" (e.g., Gal 2:16; Rom 3:28) to mean that ethics were unimportant.

Paul's response to the man having an affair with his stepmother and to lawsuits within the church focuses on the community rather than on the person having the affair or the person being cheated. He tells the church they must expel the man having sex with his stepmother in order to maintain the holiness of the community. The whole must be spared the defilement that will come to them through allowing him to remain a part of their church (5:1-13). Putting the good of the community first means that the holiness of the community is more important than the fate of one person. Similarly, believers should endure being cheated by a fellow believer rather than bring a suit in public court, because of the damage such a suit would cause to the reputation of the church (6:1-11). Such instructions implicitly return to the "word of the cross" as the pattern for living in the church, as they ask believers to do what is best for others rather than for themselves.

In response to those who are proud of the man sleeping with his stepmother and those who are having sex with prostitutes, Paul rejects the idea that bodies are unimportant. As we will see in his discussion of the resurrection, he sees bodily existence as the permanent state of humans. Thus, he demands an end to indiscriminant sexual encounters, arguing that God is concerned about the whole person. Indeed, since God's Spirit lives in believers they are temples that bear the presence of God with them wherever they go (6:19; cf. Rom 8:9-11). Profligate sex brings God into situations that violate God's holiness. In addition, sex involves the whole person, not just the body. Paul draws this assertion from Genesis 2:24, which says that the man and woman become one in marriage. Finally, he interprets the death of Jesus as the means by which God has purchased believers. Since they now belong to God, they must behave in ways that honor God—and profligate sex does not do that (6:12-20).

The other view that could grow out of seeing the body as unimportant is that it should be continually deprived to remind the person of its unimportance. Those at Corinth who think people should refrain from sex in marriage seem to hold this view. Paul's discussion of marriage reflects the discussions about it in philosophical schools. When philosophers discussed marriage, they considered what the city needed at that moment and how the philosopher could best fulfill his role as teacher and leader. If there was a need for more children, then the philosopher should marry, some said. But often, the philosopher's allegiance to a higher calling meant that he would eschew marriage so he could devote his time to duties other than family responsibilities (e.g., Epictetus, *Discourses* 3.22.69-74). Similarly, Paul sees the circumstances of his time to suggest that remaining single was preferable, but not because the body or sex was evil. Rather, it was a matter of ordering one's priorities. At that moment, he thinks, the single life better allows one to attend to the proper priorities. Paul evaluates this matter as he does because of his understanding of the eschatological moment. He sets the discussion in the context of the coming return of Christ and the increase in persecution that will precede it. Faithfulness will be easier without family responsibilities in this context. Still, he says marriage is a good thing, and the proper and holy context for sexual relations (7:1-40).

The Corinthians also debated whether believers could attend occasions held at temples of various gods and eat the food served there. This food would have been offered as sacrifices to those gods. Some think this is permissible, others think it involves participation in idolatry (8:1–11:1). In the ancient world, when someone offered a sacrifice to a god, only a small portion of it was actually burned on the altar (usually the fat and the entrails). Another portion was given to the priests to support the temple; then the rest was returned to the person who offered it. That person was free to do with it whatever he or she pleased. Often the person would have a banquet of some type. It might be an event such as a wedding reception or it might be the meal for a trade guild. If church members declined invitations to such events, they might offend their neighbors or miss out on important business opportunities. Those who think believers can go to these events believe they can go without worshiping the other god and want to maintain good relations with nonbelievers.

Paul's opening remarks suggest that he is going to agree with those who assert that they can attend. But after agreeing with their arguments, he rejects their conclusion by adding a further consideration. In essence, he interjects the "word of the cross." He contends that love should shape believers' conduct so that they privilege the good of the other person above their own good. They do this by remembering that their fellow believers are so valuable that Christ died for them (8:11). Thus, those who do not think worship is involved in attending these dinners cannot go because it might influence those who do think they will gain some benefit from the god to go and so violate their allegiance to worshiping only God. Paul then inserts an excursus that reminds them that he adopted this way of living when he refused financial support from them and took a job while also preaching (9:1-23).

When Paul resumes his direct instructions about food sacrificed to another god, more seems to be at stake than there was at the beginning. Now eating food dedicated to another god tempts believers to be unfaithful and associates them with that god. On the other hand, Paul acknowledges that all things in the world belong to God. So for meals outside temples where sacrificed food might be served, Paul recommends a "Don't ask, don't tell" policy. Believers can eat anything unless it is identified as dedicated to a god. If it is so identified they cannot eat it, so that it is plain to all that they give no allegiance to that god and accept no benefits from him or her. Thus, the discussion concludes with a return to concern for the good of the other.

The Corinthians also disagree about how to conduct the church's worship. They disagree about how women and men should dress when they lead worship. Some think women should cover their heads and men should not, others think both are free to dress as they wish (11:2-16). This argument involves a conflict in cultural expectations. Various images of people worshiping at altars to other gods show men with their heads covered. On the other hand, descriptions of women who come into contact with the spirit of a god are often said to have their hair flowing or even flying about. In nonreligious contexts, women's hair was to be controlled through either the way it was styled or with a head covering. In first-century synagogue worship, men did not cover their heads and women did. At the Corinthian church, some women who have the Spirit are inclined to let their hair be loose. This conforms to what they have known about how those in touch with a god behave.

It is important to note that the question is not whether women should lead worship. It is assumed that they do. The only question is how they and men should dress when they lead. The question is specifically about whether men and women cover their heads when they lead prayer or prophecy.[1] Paul tells the men to lead worship without a head covering and the women to lead worship with their heads covered. He initially justifies this by citing the hierarchy of the created order. Since men were created first in Genesis 2, they have higher status. But at 11:11, Paul's argument takes a radical turn. He now argues that "in the Lord," that is, within the sphere in which the church lives, mutual interdependence, not hierarchy, should structure life. Existence "in the Lord" trumps the created order, so the immediately preceding argument that supports his instructions about headwear has no basis. He finally resorts to saying that all the other churches follow the pattern he advocates, so they should too. Paul here asks the church to adopt the practice of the synagogue rather than that of pagan worshipers. His desire to maintain and emphasize the distinction between worship of God and worship of other gods may be a significant reason Paul gives this advice.

There are also problems with the Corinthians' conduct at the Lord's Supper, which would soon also be called the Eucharist. At this early time, the Supper included an entire meal. Some church members, particularly the wealthy, have been conducting themselves as they would in other settings that included meals with people from different social classes. The accepted protocol at a banquet was to have different food for different social classes. The more wealthy the person, the better the food and drink they were served. So some at the meal might have steak while others had a hamburger and some even got Spam. This is the way private banquets and even trade guilds organized meals. Some Corinthians think the church should conduct the Lord's Supper in the same manner. Those who oppose this practice have told Paul that some members have private meals at which they get drunk, while others remain hungry.

Paul reacts vehemently. He demands that they all eat the same food rather than having different food according to social class. This sameness at the meal both represents and enacts the oneness of all in the church; none can claim privilege based on social status. He crafts the tradition of Jesus's words spoken at the institution of the Supper so that the ritual includes the entire meal. Thus, the sharing cannot come only at the end but must be evident throughout the whole meal. He says that those who fail to see and embody the oneness of the body of Christ (the church) by serving everyone the same

---

1. Prophecy was a form of teaching in the Pauline churches.

food come under a curse. In fact, some have already become sick and some have died because of this violation (11:17-34).

The Corinthians' problems in worship include excesses in the exercise of spiritual gifts. Early church members believed that the Spirit mediated a variety of gifts, some ecstatic and others more rational. Two relatively common gifts, it seems, were speaking in tongues and prophecy. Speaking in tongues (or glossolalia) is an experience in which the speaker utters words that he or she does not understand and are generally understood not to be in a human language. These words may contain a message, but it can only be deciphered by a person who has the gift of interpretation of tongues. Speaking in tongues is a type of mystical experience in which one has a direct experience of the presence of God. The gift of prophecy involved receiving messages from God for the people of your church. It often had nothing to do with predicting the future; rather it was about proclaiming what God wanted the church to know or do at that moment. Some at Corinth think tongues are a superior gift, others think prophecy is. Both groups want to dominate the community's gathering for worship.

Paul's long discussion (chapters 12–14) of the use of spiritual gifts compares the church and its various members to a body and its parts. Paul argues that there is no one gift of the Spirit that all members should possess. Instead, just as the body needs different parts (hands, feet, eyes, ears, and so on), so the church needs members who have different functions. A body cannot function that is just a giant eye or tongue with no other parts. Likewise, the church cannot function without many different gifts being exercised. Paul emphasizes that God intended the church to have the different gifts; so to expect everyone to have one particular gift (whether tongues or prophecy) is to distort what God wants. Importantly, however, this diversity of gifts originates from the same Spirit and they all fit together to build up the community. While some were inclined to use their gifts for self-aggrandizement, Paul says that their legitimate function is to strengthen the community.

The famous description of love (chapter 13) really describes how church members are to use their spiritual gifts to serve the church. After this poetic chapter, Paul gives specific instructions about the use of tongues and prophecy in worship. He argues that prophecy is superior to speaking in tongues because prophecy communicates rational thought. Tongues, he says, are an important spiritual experience for the person who has that gift, but they should speak in tongues in the church only when there is an interpreter who can tell the others what has been said. Even with an interpreter is present, only two or at most three can speak at each worship service. While prophecy can strengthen the community by bringing an intelligible message, it can also be used to show off one's spirituality. So prophets are also limited to only two or at most three speaking at each worship service. He sets these limits so that everything may be done to build up the church (14:26). That is, every exercise of every gift should have the goal of helping others, not raising one's own status. Furthermore, worship is to be orderly so that it reflects the character of God, who is a God of order, not chaos (14:33, 40).

The final issue Paul takes up is the nature of postmortem existence. Some Corinthians rejected belief in the resurrection of the body, preferring to think of the afterlife as the immortality of the soul that is freed from a body. This view may have been influenced by popular Platonism that saw the body as something that held back the soul's perception of true reality and its participation in the realm of spirit. Some Corinthians think that bodies are too inferior to participate in their future life with God.

Paul thinks humans are a psycho-physical units (a view consistent with much Jewish thought of that era). Thus, to be without a body is to be less than fully human. Paul first reminds them that they believe in the resurrection of Christ. Then he argues that Christ's resurrection was bodily, but that it was not the resuscitation of a corpse. Rather, it was a transformation of his body, so that it was composed of matter that is different from the matter of this realm. Christ's resurrection was bodily, but not "flesh and blood." He lists off different kinds of bodies to demonstrate that bodies are made of different substances. He then asserts that believers' bodies will be patterned after the resurrection of Christ. Indeed, Christ's resurrection was the "first-fruits" (15:20) of the resurrection; that is, the sample of what the believer's resurrection will be. Thus, believers will be embodied, but in this new existence their bodies will be composed of matter that is different from "flesh and blood" (15:50).

Many of the problems this letter addresses seem to stem from the Corinthians' inability to adopt fully their new system of beliefs. What they had believed about how people experience gods and what they gain from that experience is brought into the church. Their prior beliefs shaped what they thought about ways to gain status in a community and about proper behavior in community. So they have mixed their earlier beliefs with what Paul taught in ways that he finds unacceptable. They had not succeeded in reshaping their cultural understandings so that they were consistent with Paul's gospel.

Watching Paul Work

Paul uses a number of strategies to persuade the Corinthians to see things his way. Some of these are well-known rhetorical strategies; others rely on distinctive theological tenets. Among the rhetorical strategies he employs is citing authorities. Of course he cites scripture. He does this more often in chapters 1–4 and 15. In 1:19, 31; 2:9; and 3:19-20 he identifies the quoted material as scripture, as he does in 15:54-55 (see also 6:16; 9:9). This ensures that his mostly Gentile readers recognize that these words come from authoritative scripture. In other places he quotes or alludes to scripture without identifying it (2:16; 8:4; 15:32). These passages may be better known or he may expect the Corinthians to hear some of them as adages of cultural wisdom. Perhaps we see this in 15:32-33 where the scriptural citation is followed immediately by a quote from the playwright Menander. In other places Paul mentions stories in the Hebrew Bible, assuming they have probative value. These include his mention of the creation story of Genesis 2 (11:8-9) and the stories of the disobedience of the Israelites in the wilderness (10:1-10).

In addition to playwrights, Paul also cites other culturally accepted ideas to bolster his arguments. He cites the laws of nature in his discussion of head coverings (11:14-15). Less directly, his metaphor of the body for the community was often used in civic discourse. Paul, however, uses this image to argue for the value of all rather than to bolster the social hierarchy, as it was usually used. His talk of factiousness as a common human failing is also a well-known topos (literary theme). Even his discussion of marriage draws on similar discussions among philosophers, as they discussed whether it was better to marry or remain single.

He relies on one other type of tradition, a saying of Jesus. When discussing the Lord's Supper, Paul cites the tradition of the Supper's institution. This oral tradition has come to Paul from earlier believers, and he shapes it here to interpret the rite and to control the way the Corinthians practice it. He assumes this tradition is authoritative. Similarly, he cites a saying of Jesus in 7:10-11. While he assumes that this saying is authoritative, he goes on to grant exceptions that the idealistic saying had not envisioned (7:15).

His strategies also include providing an elaboration of an image or belief that the Corinthians already hold so that they see new implications. He does this with the image of the church as a body. While he is not the first to elaborate this image, we have noted that he uses it to make an unexpected point.

He uses this same strategy in chapter 15. He begins his discussion of the resurrection by reminding them of what they already confess about Christ's resurrection and assuring them that their belief in it is well-grounded. He then argues that the resurrection of believers is implied by Christ's resurrection.

He also argues from his ethos, from his character. In the early parts of the letter he assures the Corinthians that he has their good as his goal. He prays for them and loves them as a parent (4:14-15). He works for their good, even when that is to his disadvantage. Even when using biting irony, he tells them how he endures hardship for them. As a trustworthy person, he is an example they should imitate (4:16; 10:33–11:1).

Use of examples is another rhetorical or argumentative strategy used throughout 1 Corinthians. Not only is Paul an example to imitate, so is Apollos. Apollos's work among the Corinthians exemplifies the behavior Paul wants them to adopt. Paul sends Timothy as another example. His conduct will remind them of Paul's "ways in Christ Jesus" (4:17). But there are also bad examples that they are to avoid. The mention of the unfaithfulness of Israelites in the wilderness is particularly vivid (10:1-5).

A central element in the argument of the entire letter is Paul's redefinition of what is advantageous. This is a common topic in deliberative speeches, speeches that try to influence people's judgments about how to act in the future. The heart of his redefinition is a shift from seeking personal advantage to seeking what is advantageous for the community or for the other person. We see this in his response to the Corinthian slogan, "All things are lawful for me" (6:12; 10:23). Each time he repeats their slogan, he modifies it by saying, "but not all things build up" (NRSV: "are beneficial"). That is, all things do not contribute to the growth of the community. In 10:24, he continues this qualification of their slogan by explicitly telling them not to seek their own good but that of their fellow believers. It is just below this exhortation that he gives himself as an example of one who gives up what is advantageous for himself in order to benefit others (10:33–11:1).

This central rhetorical goal also takes us to the central theological theme of 1 Corinthians. In the face of the Corinthians' idea that the Spirit makes people superior in ways that allow them to claim privilege and to have advantages over others, Paul asserts that the Spirit enables believers to put the good of others ahead of their own good. His case relies on their acceptance of Christ's death as the authoritative example for their lives. He contrasts the wisdom and power of humans and of "this age" with the way of Christ. The

71

central theological argument of the letter (1:18–2:16) defines the gospel as the word (or message) of the cross. Paul acknowledges that this message runs contrary to all expectations and values of the world outside the church. A message that claims that the revelation of God and the exercise of God's saving power is found in an executed insurrectionist's death sounds ridiculous. It inverts all the values and expectations of those who do not accept it. But he contends that God's wisdom is seen in Christ being willing to put the good of others before his own good, in being willing to accept disadvantage—even to the point of a shameful death—in order to provide advantages for others.

Paul argues that the "word of the cross," the story of Jesus accepting disadvantage for the good of others, is the authoritative paradigm for life in the church. The cross is the generative or originating metaphor for the church's existence and ethic. It demands a whole new way of perceiving reality. It has already determined who is in the church (1:26-31), how Paul preaches, and how he conducts his ministry (2:1-5). Now Paul contends that the cross must be the norm by which all of life is evaluated. It must shape how the Corinthians envision spirituality, how they evaluate leaders, and how they live in relation to one another.

The exemplar of the cross provides the way of viewing reality that will end the Corinthians' factious disputes by leading them to put the good of others first. Rather than seeking a teacher through whom they will gain status, they will follow those who help them give up advantage for the sake of others. Rather than seeing the Spirit as a presence that makes them impressive and dominant, Paul says the Spirit will enable them to endure the disadvantages they accept for others. This theme touches nearly every issue raised in chapters 5–15. The "word of the cross" will determine whether they bring each other into court, how they behave sexually, whether they eat food offered to another god, and how they conduct themselves in the context of communal worship. Paul uses the various types of arguments we have seen above to lead the Corinthians to recognize how their behavior needs to conform to the example set in the cross.

This pattern of life has been critiqued because calls for its adoption have been used to counsel submission to oppressive structures and abusive relationships. Such advice misuses Paul's words and advocates the opposite of what he has in mind. The pattern of the cross has the powerful Christ give up advantage to aid those in an inferior position. Paul calls the more powerful to abdicate their privilege for those with less power.

A second theological theme that threads its way throughout the letter and supports Paul's arguments is his eschatological understanding of reality. The first explicit eschatological reference comes in 1:8 where Paul mentions "the day of our Lord Jesus Christ." The "word of the cross" is an eschatological message; it is foolishness to those perishing (1:18) and it is the decisive act that signals the end of the rule of the powers that now dominate the world (2:6-8). The status of church members at the time of judgment suggests that they should be able to adjudicate claims about financial matters that arise in the church (6:2-4). Paul's evaluation of whether it is better to marry has an eschatological basis (7:29-31). Paul's treatment of head coverings and his assertion of mutuality rather than hierarchy as the proper order in the church rests on the church being a part of the new creation (11:8-12). When Paul corrects their behavior at the Lord's Supper, he reminds them that the meal proclaims the Lord's death "until he comes" (11:26). So the Lord's Supper's meaning has an eschatological aspect. Spiritual gifts, a major issue in the letter, are gifts of the eschatological time, signs of God's intimate presence. The final issue of the letter involves the nature of the resurrection. Thus throughout the letter, various issues are set in an eschatological context.

What We Learn about Paul

This letter demonstrates that the death and resurrection of Christ, as a single and inseparable event, play an important role in Paul's beliefs and in how he arrives at what he thinks the church should be and do. There is little talk of atonement as the function of Jesus's death and resurrection, but that meaning is assumed as foundational for the church (see 15:3-4). Jesus's death and resurrection has a broader function here; it exemplifies what God accomplishes through Christ. In 1 Corinthians, it is not the teaching or healing of Jesus that serves as the guide for how to live as believers; it is his death and resurrection. This complex event is central for Paul's understanding of the meaning of Jesus. The heart of what Jesus taught and did, the center of the meaning of his work, is found in his death and resurrection.

The "word of the cross," then, is central to Paul's theology. It sets the paradigm for his ministry and for the lives of believers. It determines how believers should understand leadership and life in community. Indeed, it determines all of existence. The "word of the cross" demonstrates how God acts among God's people and how they are to respond to God's gracious presence.

It is a dramatic rejection of the values that support the institutional structures of the world.

This "word of the cross" is also an eschatological proclamation. Jesus's death and resurrection are the moment at which the decisive victory over death and the powers that govern the world was achieved. Their ultimate demise and the final conformity of believers to the life of Christ are guaranteed by that death and resurrection. These events are at the very center of Paul's understanding of the faith, his understanding of God, Christ, and all of existence.

The centrality of the death and resurrection of Jesus contributes to making eschatology crucial in Paul's thinking. His theological reasoning works from the assumption that the church lives in the eschatological time. While the end of chapter 7 indicates that he thinks the end is fairly near, it is not its immediacy but its certainty that is crucial. The activity of the Spirit is decisive evidence that it is the eschatological time, even as it confirms the meaning and reality of the resurrection of Jesus. Locating the church in the eschatological time enables Paul to interpret present experience (including suffering and persecution) and to be confident in the final victory of God because it was presaged and assured by the resurrection of Christ. For Paul the exalted Christ has yet to completely defeat God's enemies (who are also the church's enemies), and so the church lives in the time between the sign that God has the power to defeat those evil powers and the final exercise of that power to reclaim all things for God's self (15:20-28).

Paul's use of the "word of the cross" as the paradigm for living means that he rejects an individualistic understanding of the gospel. The "word of the cross" exemplifies the belief that the good of the community is more important than the good of individuals. For Paul, the cross calls all believers to shift their pattern of thinking so that the community's good takes precedence over his or her own good.

Even in this most practical of letters, Paul works as a theologian; that is, he interprets the gospel for new situations. He tries to show his churches how to understand and respond to situations they encounter through the lens of the gospel. This is his mode of operation in all of his letters. The two theological themes that function most directly in 1 Corinthians (the "word of the cross" and eschatology) presuppose certain beliefs about the nature of God and Christ, about the salvation that the church is given by God in Christ, and about the nature of the community that exists in the sphere of Christ, among other things. But those beliefs play a less prominent (and often less explicit) role in the ways Paul tries to convince the Corinthians to understand all things through the eschatological "word of the cross."

Suggested Reading

Joseph A. Fitzmyer. *First Corinthians: A New Translation with Introduction and Commentary.* New Haven: Yale University Press, 2008.

Victor P. Furnish. *The Theology of the First Letter to the Corinthians.* New Testament Theology. New York: Cambridge University Press, 1999.

Richard B. Hays. *First Corinthians.* Interpretation. Louisville: Westminster John Knox, 2011.

Richard A. Horsley. *1 Corinthians.* Abingdon New Testament Commentary. Nashville: Abingdon, 1998.

Criag S. Keener. *1–2 Corinthians.* New Cambridge Bible. New York: Cambridge University Press, 2005.

Margaret E. Thrall. *The First and Second Letters of Paul to the Corinthians.* The Cambridge Bible Commentary. Cambridge: Cambridge University Press, 1965.

Chapter 7
SECOND CORINTHIANS

Redefining Leadership and Apostleship

Most interpreters think 2 Corinthians is composed of what were originally at least two different letters, and some think as many as six. However many letters there were originally, they were all written within eighteen to twenty-four months of the time of 1 Corinthians, and so all were completed no later than 56–58. Here we will assume that chapters 1–7 (and perhaps 1–9) were originally a single letter and that chapters 10–13 were a separate and later letter. (See appendix for the argument that supports this arrangement.)

This view generates the following reconstruction of events. Soon after Paul dispatched 1 Corinthians, Timothy visited Corinth (1 Cor 16:10-11). Either Timothy or another source from Corinth informed Paul of new problems. Some teachers had arrived who claimed to be apostles and cast doubt on the legitimacy of Paul's apostleship. At this news, Paul returned to Corinth, but the visit did not go well. Someone insulted him and the church did not come to his defense. Paul left, saying he would be back soon. Upon reflection, Paul did not return but instead wrote a strong letter that he says was written "with many tears" (2:1-4). Titus delivered this letter and served as Paul's representative. Some interpreters think chapters 10–13 constitute the body of this painful letter. It seems more likely, however, that the painful letter is lost.

Titus met Paul in Macedonia (northern Greece) and gave a hopeful account of the circumstances in Corinth. The church seemed to have turned back to Paul and away from the other teachers. In response to this report, Paul wrote chapters 1–7 (or possibly 1–8 or less likely 1–9). This letter continues Paul's defense of his apostleship and his conduct among the Corinthians, particularly the cancellation of his visit, but also works to mend relations with them. Thus, there are several overtures of reconciliation, even as Paul corrects their understanding of apostleship.

But Titus was overly optimistic. When Paul heard from Corinth again, they were siding more with the other teachers and doubting Paul's legitimacy. In response, Paul wrote the harsh letter of chapters 10–13. Here he chides and threatens the Corinthians, finally telling them that when he returns, he will exercise God's power in an unpleasant way if they have not rejected those other teachers and acknowledged him. We have no more record of the exchange between Paul and the Corinthians. But Romans 16:1 suggests that he reclaimed their allegiance, because he wrote Romans from Corinth and sent it by a deacon of a church in one of Corinth's harbor districts (Cenchrea). In addition, the Corinthians participated in the Collection for the Jerusalem church (Rom 15:26). Beyond those signals, in the mid- to late nineties, Clement of Rome assumed that the Corinthian church honored Paul and had preserved his letters.

The various hypotheses about the number of letters in 2 Corinthians disagree about the chronology of Paul's relations with the Corinthian church, but they make little difference in trying to understand the practical and theological issues at stake.

Practical Problems and Responses

Second Corinthians has one central issue: apostleship. The situation at Corinth demands that Paul focus attention on defining what apostles are and how they behave and on defending his claim to be one. Apparently, 1 Corinthians was not successful in changing this church's outlook. Paul argued in 1 Corinthians that the central paradigm for life as a believer is the "word of the cross." He defined this as putting the good of others and of the church ahead of one's own good, as Jesus did on the cross. Jesus accepted the disadvantage of dying a shameful death to benefit others. Now those who believe in him are to imitate that exemplar by privileging the good of others before their own good. He makes this pattern of life the heart of Christian spirituality. Despite his lengthy argument, the Corinthians continue to see powerful manifestations as the real signs of the Spirit's presence.

The new teachers and the Corinthians have the same view of the Spirit. Powerful and impressive manifestations of the Spirit are a central element of the new teachers' understanding and practice of apostleship. They say that apostles live above the troubles of life, are impressive speakers and imposing presences. These characteristics manifest the Spirit in a measure that indicates that they are apostles. They secure their positions and the allegiance of the Corinthians by displaying these abilities and criticize Paul for not manifesting these powers. Further, they say that the absence of such displays is clear evidence that Paul is not an apostle. While Paul does not take up the language of the "word of the cross" in 2 Corinthians (though he reflects that thought in 13:4), he argues that the Spirit shows itself in apostles through their willingness to suffer for the good of the church.

All of the specific problems Paul addresses in 2 Corinthians involve understanding apostleship and his claim to be an apostle. (Chapters 8 and 9 do not address problems; they give instructions about the Collection for Jerusalem.) The rival apostles accuse Paul of being unreliable because he had failed to return to Corinth when he said he would (1:15–2:2) and had instead sent the "letter of tears" (2:4). Whatever Paul said in that letter, it caused the church to punish the one who had insulted him. In fact, Paul now says they should stop punishing him because Paul sees their commitment to him (2:5-11).

Paul is in a difficult position. He must both thank the Corinthians for their new show of loyalty and defend himself against the charge of inconsistency. To accomplish both objectives he tells them how much they mean to him and asserts that he wrote the letter rather than returning in person to spare them grief.

At 2:14, Paul shifts from discussing particular incidents and their aftermath to considering the nature of apostleship directly. He begins with a shocking analogy. He says apostles are always being led "in triumphal procession." This metaphor envisions the apostle as a prisoner of war who is marched through the streets of Rome in the victory parade. At the end of the parade, these prisoners are executed. Paul says that is what it means to be an apostle. Then he shifts his metaphor so that he is a sacrifice being offered. The aroma of the sacrifice brings life to those who believe his message, but death to those who do not. This combination of images means that the apostle both accepts suffering and wields great power. That is a strange combination—especially in the eyes of the Corinthians. Importantly, Paul asserts that he does not pretend to be qualified for such an office; indeed, no one could be. On the other hand, he says that God makes him able to fulfill this ministry.

Paul asserts his superiority by noting that his rivals need recommendations. They brought letters of recommendation from other churches, but not him. After all, there was no church in Corinth to read a letter when Paul arrived. So rather than bringing a letter, their church's existence is his letter. Thus, while his opponents have human recommendations, he has a recommendation from God (3:1-3). Mention of letters leads Paul to contrast things written on stone with things written on the heart. This, in turn, leads him to contrast his ministry with the ministry of Moses, the one who received the commandments written on stone. Paul says the ministry of Moses was glorious; it brought Moses into the presence of God. Yet being an apostle of Christ is even more glorious. This is a claim the Corinthians might be interested in.

But just as it seems they may get what they want, Paul argues that this glory is seen in suffering for others. The message and the ministry are glorious, but the apostle is a disposable paper cup (4:7).[1] Suffering and weakness characterize apostles' lives, not power and glory. God arranged things in this way to make it clear that the power is God's not the apostle's. This takes us to the heart of the disagreement. The Corinthians and their new apostles want God's power to make apostles (and all believers) impressive. Paul rejects this paradigm, asserting that the weakness of the apostle makes it obvious that a power that is not his own works in him. Thus, honor is given to God, not the apostle.

Paul also describes the apostolic office as a ministry of reconciliation. In the middle of a conflict, Paul says his calling is to proclaim that in Christ God is reconciling the world to Godself (5:18-21). The reconciliation to God that Paul proclaims also demands that the Corinthians be reconciled to Paul. The church's relationship with the apostle is an element of its acceptance of reconciliation with God. The church must accept God's authorized representative. Thus, their commitment to Paul is an element of their acceptance of the gift of God.

In chapter 7, Paul recounts the Corinthians' acceptance of him and his apostolate. They have turned from his rivals and their theology of apostleship

1. Paul actually says "clay jar." That was the cheap disposable drinking cup of the first century.

and have renewed their relationship with him. So he can rejoice. If chapter 8 (or chapters 8 and 9) are a part of the same letter as 1–7, then Paul assumes that he has made a strong enough case that he can ask them to fulfill their commitment to participate in the collection for Jerusalem.

When the letter of 10–13 opens, the Corinthians' criticism of Paul has gotten sharper. He is now accused of inconsistency not just in the way he makes plans but also in his behavior generally. Some say he is bold and demanding at a safe distance when writing letters, but weak in person. They portray this perceived difference as cowardice (10:1-11). The rival apostles, on the other hand, claim to be "of Christ" in a sense that gives them authority and power. They question whether Paul possesses this status. In response, Paul threatens to exercise power to put them in their place when he gets there (10:11).

He chides his rivals for bragging about meeting standards they set for themselves rather than standards he or God recognize. He, on the other hand, points to the Corinthians and other churches he has started as evidence of his apostolic credentials and power.

The central part of this letter is the "Fool's Speech" (11:1–12:13). Paul asks the Corinthians to let him behave as a fool because they love fools. He mocks his rivals' claims, contending that they do not care about the Corinthians but only their own advancement and power. Paul portrays them as abusively authoritarian and as people who constantly brag about their superior accomplishments and spiritual powers. They claim their Jewish heritage as a mark of authority in this Gentile church and combine that with a claim to be "servants of Christ" in a sense that gives them authority over the church (11:23). They also brag about spiritual experiences and the power they gain through them.

Paul presents himself as the opposite of such self-serving rivals. If they claim to be apostles because of the power evident in their successful and impressive lives, Paul claims to be an apostle because he suffers and is abused to benefit his churches—especially the Corinthians. His willingness to accept difficulties and even to disadvantage himself by working as a laborer is evidence of his love for them and the genuineness of his apostleship; it is evidence that the power of God works in him. He does have superior spiritual experiences, but rejects the idea that they are evidence of apostleship. While they have seen him exercise power (12:12), he does not use it to usurp authority.

Throughout this letter Paul urges the Corinthians to shift their perspective so that they see the power of God in willingness to disadvantage oneself for the good of others rather than in the ability to seize power. His refusal of financial support from them is an example of his willingness to accept disadvantage for their good, even as his rivals use accepting support to express dominance. As he closes the letter, however, he threatens the church and his rivals with a show of God's power that will demonstrate his genuineness and his rivals' falseness if they do not repent (13:1-4).

Watching Paul Work

Since 2 Corinthians has material that addresses at least two stages in the relationship between Paul and this church, it contains a wide range of types of persuasion and even some different tones of voice. The facts on the ground are not in question. Everyone in the dispute agrees about what Paul has done and about what the rival teachers do. The question is, *What do those actions mean?* Everyone knows that Paul said he would return but that he had not. The rivals interpret his failure to return as unreliability and cowardice. So he reframes the discussion, arguing that he stayed away out of love for them. Here, and in many places in 2 Corinthians, Paul presents himself as the kind of person they should trust. That is, he develops his ethos. Ancient rhetoricians argued that one of the most important things a speaker could do was to convince the audience that he was a person who had its good at heart. Conversely, speakers should argue that their opponents were not the types of people you should trust.

Rhetoricians also agreed that one of the best ways to develop a good image of oneself was to talk about the troubles you had endured for the good of your audience. Conforming to this advice, Paul explains how much he suffers for the church. He gives extensive lists of what he has endured for the church and the gospel. These hardship catalogues (4:8-9; 6:4-10) demonstrate both Paul's superior character and the value of the gospel. As they demonstrate Paul's character, these lists also evoke pity. Paul often tries to reach the Corinthians at the level of emotions. Again, rhetoricians recommend that speakers evoke certain emotions in their audience because emotions influence how people make judgments about the meanings of events. Thus, Paul wants the Corinthians to have certain feelings about him so they will interpret the facts as he wants them to.

Another fact that everyone agrees about is that Paul's demeanor is different from that of his rivals. His explanation for adopting his strange manner of life again reframes the issue so that his willingness to suffer is an expression of love for them (4:15; 6:11-12; 7:2-3). He again contrasts this with his rivals who have impure motives and take advantage of the Corinthians (2:17). In this instance too, then, he presents himself as one who has their good at heart, even as he discredits his rivals.

Another way Paul reframes the discussion is by denying that he is commending himself (3:1; 5:12). He contrasts his giving the Corinthians an opportunity to be proud of him with the bragging that the rivals do about themselves. Thus, Paul again works for the good of the Corinthians while the rivals engage in self-aggrandizement.

Paul uses a number of other persuasive devices. On occasion he cites scripture (4:13). In 3:1-18, Paul compares his ministry with the ministry of Moses. Even when the scripture does not establish a central point, its citation gives weight to his argument. He also draws in the Corinthians with dramatic imagery; for example, he speaks of death living in him, so that he brings life to them (4:10-12). We saw above the dramatic image of the apostle as the prisoner of war about to be executed (2:14). Importantly, throughout 1–7 Paul expresses confidence in the readers. His approval nurtures the bond between him and them.

In chapters 10–13, the severity of the problem leads Paul to use different kinds of arguments. This letter is full of irony and sarcasm. Paul's boast of weakness rather than strength (e.g., 11:30) is a prominent example. Irony opens the letter as Paul accepts the indictment that his personal presence lacks the power that should accompany the office of apostle, even though he is plenty bold when safely far away and writing letters. Then after claiming that his presence reflects the "meekness and gentleness of Christ" (10:1), he adds—to make the charge sound ridiculous—that he wants to avoid frightening them with this letter (10:9-11). The sarcasm is palpable when he apologizes for being too weak to abuse the church as his rivals do (11:20-21). The sarcasm even leans toward mockery when he calls the rivals "super-apostles" (11:5) and concludes his chiding of them for only evaluating themselves with standards they make up by saying, "They do not show good sense" (10:12-13). Perhaps we catch the tone with the paraphrase, "They're just being stupid."

The entire Fool's Speech has an ironic tone. As Paul pretends to meet their criteria for evaluating apostles, he really emphasizes differences in practices and in motives. Within this speech he also resorts to parody in his report of an unnamed person who has a vision so wonderful that he is not allowed to tell about it. But rather than bringing him power and something to brag about (the use his rivals make of such experiences), his superior visions bring him more suffering so that he will not become arrogant—as his rivals have (12:1-10). He goes so far as to identify these rivals with Satan (11:3; cf. 11:12-15).

At the beginning and end of 10–13, Paul threatens the Corinthians with an exercise of God's power that will administer discipline (10:8-11; 13:1-3, 10). This is not the intended use of this power. Yet, to keep them from a false understanding of the faith that would severe their ties with the true apostle and the genuine gospel, Paul will use it.

Paul has such difficulty defeating these rivals because 1 Corinthians did not convince its readers that the "word of the cross" should be the pattern for the church's life and spirituality. They question Paul's qualifications for apostleship precisely because he follows this pattern of accepting disadvantage for the good of others. So in 2 Corinthians he develops the "word of the cross" image by pairing it with the resurrection. The shape of this elaboration is explicit in 13:4, the only mention of the crucifixion in 2 Corinthians. Here he says Christ was crucified in weakness but lives by the power of God. Paul's life follows this pattern: He lives in weakness but will live with Christ by the power of God. Rather than referring to the cross, in the letters of 2 Corinthians Paul talks about weakness and power, with death and resurrection as the dominant metaphor. This theological metaphor supports the letter's central theological assertion about legitimate claims to possessing divine power.

The change of the metaphor from "word of the cross" to death and resurrection helps Paul talk about the relationship between weakness and power that he wants the Corinthians to see in his apostleship. He uses this image in two ways. One is what we see in 13:4: Power comes after a time of weakness. The apostle accepts disadvantage and persecution but will receive life with God after death. This follows the pattern of Jesus who accepted disadvantage and death during his ministry and passion, but was raised by God. This is also the perspective in 4:17–5:5, where Paul says that if he is killed he knows he will live with God. This is not, however, the dominant use of the death/resurrection image.

In strategic places in both 1–7 and 10–13, Paul speaks of weakness and power appearing simultaneously in his apostolic labors. At the letter's beginning he speaks of enduring the sufferings of Christ, while simultaneously having consolation from God in the midst of those sufferings. More than this, Paul's afflictions bring consolation and salvation to the Corinthians (1:5-6). So God's power is at work in Paul's suffering in such a powerful way that it not only helps him endure but also makes Paul's sufferings mediate salvation to others.

At 2:14, the start of a major section of the letter, the triumphal procession metaphor utilizes the same pattern. Paul's apostolic suffering mediates the "aroma of Christ," God's saving power. Thus, again apostolic weakness is the occasion of the working of God's power.

After extolling the glory of the new covenant, Paul makes certain that his readers do not conclude that such glory means that apostles have glorious lives. First, he identifies himself as their slave (4:5). Then he says he is the cheap disposable container that brings the priceless gospel to others. This image indicates that he is weak, so that it is obvious that only the power of God enables their experience of God. Paul is always clear that God's power, not Jesus's own power, raised Jesus. So the analogy holds: God's power works through Paul's suffering just as it worked through the death and resurrection of Jesus. He is even more graphic in 4:10-12. As Paul suffers he carries around the death of Jesus, but simultaneously believers see the life of Jesus in Paul's suffering and so receive life from God as Jesus did in the resurrection. Paul's apostolic suffering is an embodiment of the gospel that has Jesus's death and resurrection at its core.

In 10–13, Paul constantly reinterprets his suffering. When explaining why he rejects asserting power and dominance as appropriate behaviors within the church, he says his extraordinary spiritual experiences have not given him power that makes him look impressive but have led to suffering a "thorn in the flesh" (12:7). He argues that this must be the pattern for apostles and ministers of Christ. They must accept weakness because it is in their weakness that God's power is seen most clearly; the more Paul accepts weakness, the more clearly God's power is visible (12:8-10).

The basic theological assertion undergirding this argument is that there must be a parallel between the death and resurrection of Jesus and the lives of apostles and leaders of the church. The entire argument of 2 Corinthians (really of all the Corinthian correspondence) is built on this foundation. This is, of course, a countercultural understanding of leadership and of what the presence of God does in a person's life. While religions of the Greco-Roman world see experiences of God as encounters that bring a person power and prestige, Paul says that the gospel brings an experience of God that shows itself in willingness to suffer for the good of others. This is not what most people hoped for as they sought an experience of a god. Perhaps we can see why the rival apostles had some success among the Corinthians.

In addition to this central theme, Paul builds on other related theological foundations to support his call for the Corinthians to acknowledge him and reject his rivals. Two important themes are interwoven in chapter 5. Paul concludes his discussion of his certainty of receiving life after apostolic toils by reminding the readers that everyone must face judgment (5:10). He then says that he is a missionary because wants others to be ready for God's judgment. Further, his service to them should give them reason to be proud of him at judgment (5:11-13). Even this line of thought circles back to the death and resurrection of Christ. His death for believers enables them to stand in judgment and to live for others. Thus, Christ's death and resurrection give assurance about the future and demands a particular way of life now. Thus, Paul moves from talking about future elements of eschatology to reflecting on how the in-breaking of the end time should shape believers' lives in the present.

Verses 16-21 develop that eschatological theme to address how believers should evaluate apostles: The presence of the end time means that all values have been altered. The change is so dramatic that Paul says there is a new creation. To retain the usual way of evaluating things is to view things "from a human point of view" (NRSV), more literally, "according to the flesh" (5:16-18). This new way of viewing things is a part of living the new life that comes through the death of Christ; that is, it is a part of being in the church, part of living in the sphere in which Christ rules. The implication is that the Corinthians should evaluate Paul's ministry, and that of his rivals, according to criteria of the new creation rather than their current standards that conform to the old world.

Paul argues that this new world comes to believers because God has reconciled the world to Godself through Christ. This metaphor for how God is present and saves assumes that humans were estranged from God, that they had rejected God and God's will. In spite of that, God seeks them out and reestablishes a loving relationship through Christ. Paul's mission, then, is to tell others about that reconciliation. So Paul calls the Corinthians to be reconciled to God (5:19-21). A consequence of their acceptance of reconciliation with

God is that they must also be reconciled to Paul. Their openness to him is the appropriate response to God's reconciling activity and Paul's proclamation of it (6:11-13). Thus, both their participation in the eschatological time and the gift of reconciliation demand that they accept him as the genuine apostle.

Throughout 2 Corinthians, Paul cites things the Corinthians already believe, things he likely taught them, to convince them to side with him. They believe that the death and resurrection of Jesus are important, so he argues that those events set the pattern for genuine apostleship and ministry—and he would say, all of life. They believe that their experience of the presence of God in the Spirit is an aspect of participating in the last days, so Paul says their standards of evaluating apostles and all things must conform to the new age, not the values of those who remain outside of God's realm. When he says that they are the new creation because God reconciled them to Godself, he expects their treatment of one another, and especially of him, to mirror what God has done for them. So they must be reconciled to Paul. Paul does little to establish these theological points; he assumes they share these beliefs. His basic methodological assumption is that the lives of believers are to be shaped by the gospel and what God has done for them through it. His task is to lead them to see and accept implications they had not recognized so they can live fully in the life that message gives and demands.

What We Learn about Paul

In many ways, 2 Corinthians is a continuation of the debate Paul engaged in 1 Corinthians. The issue continues to be how to evaluate leaders and how the Spirit manifests itself in leaders and believers. While the language Paul uses changes, a foundational element of his theology that is at work is the death and resurrection of Jesus. Paul understands these events as the means by which God reestablishes a right relationship with humanity, but this is not the primary use he makes of them in the Corinthian correspondence. Their central function is as the exemplar for life as a believer. Christ's death and resurrection set the pattern for the lives of leaders, including apostles, and for all believers.

This radical assertion about proper behavior seems to be a constant in Paul's theological reflections. It is so important because it is based on the defining element of the work of Christ: his death and resurrection. For Paul's theological reasoning, everything has to be reevaluated through the lens of

Christ's death and resurrection. That event is the primary way God and God's will are known. The eschatological nature of the event also makes it crucial in his thought. It signals that God has begun reclaiming the cosmos. Believers are brought into, reborn into, that new creation. Participation in this new era means rejecting the values of the old era. The Corinthian correspondence is Paul's attempt to get these readers to understand how participating in the eschatological era should change how a person behaves and how they should evaluate leaders and all things.

We again, then, see the eschatological nature of Jesus's death and resurrection as central elements in the ways Paul constructs his instructions to his churches, thinks about God, and interprets the world. These letters try to draw the Corinthians into viewing things through that same lens.

In a group of letters that emphasize apostleship and in which Paul is exercising authority, he still gives reasons for following his instructions. He does not assume that his word as an apostle is sufficient reason for the Corinthians to do as he says. This is not just because his apostleship is under attack. Throughout Paul's letters he gives his readers reasons to accept his understanding of various issues. He does this at least in part because of his pneumatology. He thinks that the Spirit in each believer enables each to discern the will of God. They may also need outside help, but the Spirit grants insight and transforms each believer into the image of Christ (3:15-18). This is one more aspect of life in the eschatological era.

Suggested Reading

Ernest Best. *Second Corinthians.* Interpretation. Louisville: Westminster John Knox, 2012 (reprint of 1987 edition).

Raymond F. Collins. *Second Corinthians.* Paideia. Grand Rapids: Baker Academic, 2013.

Victor P. Furnish. *II Corinthians: A New Translation with Introduction and Commentary.* New York: Doubleday, 1984.

Craig S. Keener. *1–2 Corinthians.* New Cambridge Bible. New York: Cambridge University Press, 2005.

Frank J. Matera. *II Corinthians: A Commentary.* New Testament Library. Louisville: Westminster John Knox, 2003.

Jerome Murphy-O'Connor. *The Theology of the Second Letter to the Corinthians*. New Testament Theology. New York: Cambridge University Press, 1991.

Calvin Roetzel. *2 Corinthians*. Abingdon New Testament Commentaries. Nashville: Abingdon, 2007.

Margaret E. Thrall. *The First and Second Letters of Paul to the Corinthians*. The Cambridge Bible Commentary. Cambridge: Cambridge University Press, 1965.

Chapter 8

GALATIANS

What Are We to Do with Gentiles?

Galatians has one issue in view and attention to that matter never lapses. That issue is whether Gentiles in the church should be circumcised and observe some Jewish holy days. That is, its topic is how Gentiles keep the law. As we noted in chapter 4, this was one of the most hotly debated issues of the first five or six decades of the church's existence. Galatians deals directly and forcefully with this question. While interpreters differ about the details of the debate, all agree that circumcision for Gentile believers is the basic issue.

The recipients of this letter are the churches of Galatia. Galatia may designate the ancient region of Galatia or the Roman province of Galatia. While the region of Galatia is in the middle and northern parts of Asia Minor (today's Turkey), the Roman province extended farther south so that in places it was only about 50 miles from Turkey's southern coast. Most interpreters think the letter was written to the northern region around 54–56, though some opt for the southern area and a date of 48–50.

Practical Problems and Responses

Galatians is more fiercely combative than any other of Paul's letters (with the possible exception of 2 Cor 10–13). He is graphic in his rejection of the other teachers (e.g., 5:12) and sharp in his criticisms of the letter's recipients (e.g., 3:1). He thinks that the issues being contested should have been resolved by previous debates.

The other teachers, whom Paul calls "agitators" (5:12), urge the Gentiles in these churches to be circumcised (5:2-6; 6:12-13) and to observe Jewish holy days (4:10). But these agitators do not seem to expect Gentiles converts to keep all of the law in the ways that Jews do. When Paul declares that those who accept circumcision are obliged to keep the whole law (5:3), he says it as though it is news to the readers. These agitators seem to claim that their teaching is the same as Paul's, because he has to deny that he teaches that Gentiles should be circumcised (5:11). So they do not oppose Paul's apostleship or authority. Many earlier interpreters read Paul's remarks about his life that tell of being a persecutor and of his confrontation with Peter at Antioch (1:11–2:14) as a defense of his apostleship. But those stories serve instead to establish Paul's character as trustworthy and as one who has always argued that Gentiles must not accept circumcision as an expectation of church membership. This helps him reject the notion that he preaches circumcision.

Paul does not say what the agitators claim is gained by circumcision. It is not clear that they claim these observances are required for salvation. They may have presented them as moving toward perfection in the faith. Perhaps more likely is that they say it will enhance fellowship with observant Jewish members of the church and decrease the difficulties those Jewish members experience in their relations with Jews who are not in the church. This may be why one of Paul's accusations against the agitators is that they want to avoid persecution (6:11-14). Even if they only see something practical in their urgings, Paul thinks that big theological issues are at stake.

Paul contends that the Galatian Gentiles must not accept circumcision under any conditions. In fact, he threatens that any Gentile who submits to circumcision nullifies God's grace (2:21), questions God's promises (3:17-18), and loses all benefits they gained through belief in Christ (5:4). This does not, however, mean that the law is bad. Indeed, believers must fulfill the whole law by following the command to love their neighbors as they love themselves (5:13-14).

Paul's most basic response to the agitators' demands is that salvation is in Christ without the works of the law. This means that Gentiles do not need and must not accept those demands. All of the other responses Paul gives to these demands are rooted in this central assertion about how believers receive and maintain salvation. This is the theological claim that grounds all that we hear in Galatians. This claim is near the heart of Paul's theological system. Compromise here, for Paul, would invalidate his understanding of the way God has acted in Christ to bring salvation to all people.

Watching Paul Work

Paul uses a wide range of arguments in Galatians. The opening paragraph sets out the topic and tone of the letter. Paul first uses a formula for beginning a letter of reprimand, saying, "I am astonished" at how quickly they have turned from his teaching. Then he threatens them with a curse (1:8-9). Such curses may seem strange to us, but are not unknown in other ancient literature (see e.g., 1 QS 2.5-17 from the Dead Sea Scrolls) and are even recommended by rhetoricians as a good way to begin in some situations (Quintilian 4.1.20-22).

Paul devotes 1:11–2:14 to establishing his ethos as the one the Galatians should listen to. He reminds them that God commissioned him to preach specifically to Gentiles (1:16). And while he did not get his gospel from the Jerusalem apostles, they fully recognize his commission and message (1:18–2:10). He even publicly opposed Peter, his mission partner Barnabas, and his home church to protect non-Torah observant Gentile church members from being counted as lesser members of the people of God (2:10-14). So, in contrast to the agitators, Paul is willing to suffer to protect them. In fact, he suffers with them as a mother in labor. As the mother who is birthing them into identity with Christ, he wants to change his tone from reprimand to something more mild (4:18-20). Since Paul is the one who loves them and wants the best for them, they should listen to him.

On the other hand, Paul presents the advocates of the other teaching as self-serving and unreliable. They "trouble" you (NRSV: "are confusing you") and cause dissention (1:7). They want to claim the Galatians, not for the Galatians' good but only for bragging rights (4:17). They have turned the Galatians from the truth that brings salvation. They are a contagion that needs to be thrown out before they infect the rest of the group. Their troubling of these churches is so bad that they stand under God's judgment and deserve to be castrated (5:7-12). If that is not bad enough, they are cowards. The *only* reason they advocate the position they take is to avoid persecution, the persecution Paul gladly accepts for the readers' benefit (6:12-13). By the time

Paul has finished describing them, they are certainly not the people you can trust to tell you the truth.

Paul also uses arguments from pathos (emotion). In 1:6-7, Paul not only reprimands, he also expresses love. He worries that the Galatians are being troubled by a message that threatens to separate them from God's grace. In 4:12-20, Paul reminds them of the love they have shown him. Then he concludes the letter with a description of himself that is sure to arouse pity and assure them of his love for them. He says they must stop causing him problems because he bears "the marks of Jesus" in his body; that is, he has scars to show that he has suffered for the cause he defends in the letter (6:17).

While these arguments involving character and emotions incline the Galatians to listen to Paul, he also develops more intellect-based reasons for accepting his view. One way Paul establishes his case is by citing authorities that support it. He begins by citing the highest authority, God. In the greeting Paul says that his position as apostle was given him by Christ and God (1:1). Then in 1:11-12, he asserts that his teaching is from God. It came from a revelation, not from a human source. He brings together his claim to the office of apostle and his message in 1:15-17. God calls him to preach to Gentiles, and he does not consult with any other authorities in the church about it. This direct divine commission suggests that his view is correct.

Paul also uses scripture as an authority. Genesis 15:6 supports a crucial aspect of his argument (3:6). This text says that God considered Abraham righteous because of his faith. Paul's quotation of Genesis 12:3, then, connects Abraham and Gentiles, contending that Gentiles are saved in the same way Abraham was.

A conflation of Deuteronomy 27:26 and 28:58 supports his assertion that Torah observance will bring the Galatian Gentiles curse rather than blessing (3:10-14). Leviticus 18:5 lends further evidence. Then he uses Deuteronomy 21:23 to argue that Christ's crucifixion transfers to Christ the curse due to those who do not keep the law perfectly. This, he argues, is what brings the blessing of Abraham to those who have faith. Paul uses the wording of Genesis 12:7 (and related passages) to identify Christ as the singular descendant of Abraham who is the inheritor of the blessing that Paul interprets as salvation (3:15-18). The allegory of Hagar and Sarah (4:21-31) combines the overall story about these women and Abraham with the citation of some specific texts. Contrary to the literal meaning of the stories, Paul's allegory identifies Gentiles as the true heirs of the promise to Abraham.

Paul also uses scripture to support his ethical exhortations. Believers are to show love for one another because that fulfills the command that summarizes the whole law, "Love your neighbor as yourself" (Lev 19:18). If this church knows the tradition that says Jesus named this as the most important commandment, Paul's exhortation not only draws on the authority of scripture but also on that of Jesus.

Paul uses scripture in these various ways because everyone involved recognizes scripture as an authority. Thus, it is a powerful tool as he seeks to persuade the Galatians to reject the other teaching.

A third authority that Paul cites is the pattern of Abraham's life. All Jews saw Abraham as a paradigm for the way God deals with God's people. Citing an ancient venerable person as the pattern for how one should live in the present was a common strategy in the first century. The other teachers may also have claimed Abraham as proof that they were correct. After all, he was the first to be circumcised as a sign of the covenant with God. Paul makes the opposite point, arguing that Abraham was considered righteous before circumcision and so shows that Gentiles are saved without it.

Another strategy Paul employs to turn the Galatians away from the other teaching is to reinterpret the acts they are contemplating. While the other teachers say circumcision and observance of Jewish holy days provide some advantage, Paul identifies those acts as a step backward. In 4:8-11, he says that if Gentiles observe Jewish festivals, it is the equivalent of turning back to practices connected with the worship of other gods. Rather than drawing them closer to God or identifying them more clearly with God's people, observance of these festivals moves them away from God.

Paul also employs comparison: he compares elements of Torah observance with things he finds more valuable. In 5:6, it is not circumcision that matters but "faith working through love." In 6:15, the important thing is not circumcision but the "new creation"; that is, participating in the eschatological reality initiated in Christ. Still, loving one's neighbor actually fulfills the whole law. So as Paul thinks about it, *Gentiles* do not need to be circumcised and keep the law's holy days in order to fulfill the law. With a subtle but important shift, Paul says that helping one another fulfills the "law of Christ" (6:2). Here he retains the importance of the law as a way to know how to please God, but shifts where believers find that law.

Perhaps the most powerful tool he uses to convince the Galatians not to follow the other teaching is the radical opposition he sets up between being saved through Christ and being saved by keeping the law. As we will see below, he makes this contrast as stark as he can, even overstating the case to make his point. This contrast is a prominent feature in the central argument of the letter. It rises to prominence in 2:15-21 and remains a pronounced feature through 5:6.

For Paul, this debate about whether all believers need to be fully within Judaism in order to be full church members takes us to a core element of the church's identity. He identifies the church as the sphere of salvation. Those who are in the church are God's people, those who are in right relationship with God and who enjoy the blessings of salvation that those outside do not possess. To require Torah observance that identifies a person fully with the synagogue violates this meaning of the church in Paul's view. His demand that Jews and Gentiles eat together as the church demonstrates that being a member of the church must be the believer's primary religious identity. Both the nature of the church and of what Christ's death and resurrection have accomplished are at stake for Paul. So he brings forward crucial theological justifications for his position.

In 2:15-21, Paul sets out the central thesis of the letter, that believers are made righteous in Christ, not by the works of the law. This is not a contrast between faith and works, but between faith/faithfulness and works *of the law*. Paul asserts two things that everyone involved presumably agrees with: No one is justified by the works of the law and believers are justified by their connection with Christ. From these two premises Paul surmises that Gentiles do not need to convert fully to Judaism to be fully members of the church. He draws this conclusion as though it is inescapable, but it is not really the only conclusion one might draw.

This conclusion presupposes several other beliefs. Important among those beliefs is that Christ brings a new basis for membership within God's people, a new way of being that granted a covenant relationship with God. Pauline scholars are divided over what Paul means when he asserts that this relationship is secured through *pistis (Iēsou) Christou* (2:16, where it appears twice). This phrase is most commonly translated "faith in (Jesus) Christ," but the meanings of the words and the grammar of the phrase can equally well be translated, "faithfulness of (Jesus) Christ." (Notice the footnotes in the NRSV at 2:16.) If it means "faith in Christ," then it means that God grants right relationship to someone because they believe in Christ. If it means "faithfulness of Christ," then it emphasizes that a person is granted relationship with God because Christ was faithful and obedient to God's will.

In Paul, faith never means simply giving assent to a set of beliefs. Faith includes both trusting that certain things are true and adopting an orientation of life that reflects those professed beliefs. In 2:15-21, Paul seems to say that those with faith (that attitude of trust and dependence) are justified through the faithful obedience of Christ. This emphasizes the contrast between the righteousness that comes through one's own obedience to the law and that which comes through Christ's obedience. Others in the church disputed the necessity of opposing those two, but Paul sets them out as irreconcilable opposites.

The series of proofs in 3:1–4:31 supports this theological position. Paul's first proof that justification comes through Christ rather than through Torah observance is that the Galatians have already received the Spirit (3:1-6). Paul's assumption is that God's Spirit only lives in those who enjoy the proper relationship with God, those who have been justified. Since they already possess the Spirit, they must already be in right relationship with God. And since they got it without circumcision, Paul says this alone demonstrates the correctness of his position.

Paul's second theological argument is that the justification of Gentiles without circumcision fulfills God's promise that Abraham would be a blessing to all nations. Part of this fulfillment is that the nations receive the blessing in the same way that Abraham did. Abraham was blessed by God because he trusted (had faith in) God. Abraham's relationship with God could not have been related to the law because the law was not given for hundreds of years after his time. Gentile Christ believers have a relationship with God through trusting God, and it is not dependent upon Torah observance, just as Abraham's was not. So if readers accept the premise that Abraham is a pattern for the way God deals with God's people, then Torah observance cannot establish or maintain a covenant relationship with God for Gentiles.

Paul's third central theological argument is drawn from the church's tradition. He cites a baptismal liturgy. The liturgy that appears in 3:27-28 seems to be well known in Pauline congregations because references to and versions of it appear in other letters (1 Cor 7:17-20; Col 3:11). The liturgy asserts that in baptism one takes on the identity of Christ. All who are identified with Christ become the children of Abraham because Christ is the one true heir of Abraham. They do not, then, need circumcision to be children of Abraham and so receive the promised relationship with God. Paul again relies on the Galatians' experience of the Spirit as proof of their new identity and of the absence of any need for circumcision (3:26–4:7).

These three theological arguments bear the most weight in this letter. Since the basic point of the letter is to demonstrate that Gentile believers in Christ do not need and must not accept circumcision and fuller conversion into Judaism, Paul frames the discussion by opposing the "works of the law" to trusting in the faithfulness of Christ (2:15-16). While this opposition may be overdrawn, it is the way Paul wants these readers to think about the issue at this moment. Identifying Abraham as an exemplar and interpreting baptism as identification with Christ are indispensable theological arguments here. Perhaps the most powerful proof is the Galatians' own experience of the Spirit of God—and it is something they cannot deny. Their experience of the Spirit plays a prominent role throughout the letter's argument. Their possession of the Spirit by itself should be sufficient evidence that they do not need circumcision and the other demands the agitators make. Possession of the Spirit is also a part of the blessing of Abraham (3:14). Further, the Spirit is confirmation that baptism makes believers children of Abraham and so children of God (4:6-7). The Spirit also is the guide for how they are to live their lives (5:16-26). So Paul's interpretation of their experience of the Spirit plays a crucial role in this letter.

Paul sometimes overstates contrasts in Galatians to make his point. We can tell that he exaggerates at some places because we hear him discuss the same points in a more balanced way in Romans. So how Paul talks about the relationship between the law and faith in Christ in Galatians is clearly influenced by the context he is addressing.

What We Learn about Paul

Galatians confirms the importance Paul places on his experience of the risen Christ as the foundation of his call to be the apostle to the Gentiles. That vision turned him from being a persecutor to being a propagator of the faith that the church proclaimed. By this time, he also sees that vision as evidence that his gospel is true. The polemical setting of Galatians leads Paul to emphasize his independence of other teachers, including the apostles, but a moment's reflection suggests that the core of what Paul preached was already what the church proclaimed. It was the content of what the church taught that made Paul a persecutor. After his Damascus Road experience, he believed that what they said about Jesus was true.

It is impossible to know precisely what Paul opposed so vehemently in the early church's teaching. Still some things seem clear enough. First, the church's claim that Jesus was the messiah would not be enough to provoke such persecution. Several people in this era had claimed to be the messiah who would deliver Judea from Roman domination. While their movements were crushed by the Romans, we have no evidence that they inflamed persecution from within Judaism. The definition of the messiah that the church promoted combined with the proclamation of Jesus's resurrection may have been enough to incite persecution. The claim that Jesus was the initiator of the eschatological age and the mediator of its blessings may well have been provocative enough to elicit opposition.

Given the shape of Paul's own ministry and his pursuit of church members outside of Palestine, it also seems likely that part of the church's proclamation already involved the inclusion of Gentiles among the people of God. Admitting Gentiles as full members of the synagogue and full members of God's people without requiring them to become proselytes smacked of abandoning the law as the guide for how God's people should live to be faithful to the covenant. In addition, the congregation that first called Paul to be its missionary, the church at Antioch, was already a mixed congregation when Paul arrived. So he was not the first to think that the work of Christ brought Gentiles fully into the church and the people of God without adopting circumcision and other elements of the law that were required of proselytes.

Galatians shows us that both the eschatological interpretation of the life, death, and resurrection of Jesus and the full membership of Gentiles in the church are foundational elements of Paul's gospel. The eschatological interpretation of Jesus significantly reorients Paul's understanding of religious life. It means that a new approach to the law is required. It means that God has initiated a new covenant that includes Gentiles as Gentiles. It means that the proper central religious identity that gives access to the end-time blessings of God is church membership and so belief in the risen Christ as inaugurator of the end time. While Paul does not stop being a faithful Jew, he does enter a new religious community.

Galatians indicates that for Paul the church's experience of the Spirit is indisputable confirmation of the eschatological interpretation of Christ and of the membership of Gentiles. Paul says it is the only proof they need of the fullest relationship with God (3:1). Emphasis on the Spirit has been a regular element in the letters we have examined. The topic comes up in the Corinthian correspondence because exercise of spiritual gifts has become a problem, but Paul is the one who inserts the Spirit into the conversation in Galatians. So it seems clear that the Spirit plays a significant role in Paul's understanding of God and Christian existence; it is a crucial element in his belief system and in the way he interprets the gospel in various contexts (that is, in his theologizing).

Galatians also demonstrates that Paul's thinking about the place of the law has been radically reconfigured because of his belief in Christ. He talks about it as a temporary measure and as something intended only for Jews, but he still thinks that all of God's people must "fulfill" the law, even as they do not adhere to all of its commandments. Gentiles must not submit to circumcision, or they exclude themselves from salvation in Christ (5:2-4). Yet they are to follow the command to love their neighbors as themselves (5:13-15). This tension is evident in 1 Corinthians as well. Paul says in that letter that circumcision is unimportant, but obeying the commandments is everything (7:19-20). Of course, circumcision is one of the commandments! It is not as simple as saying that Paul thinks Gentiles do not need to follow the ritual laws. Paul thinks believers should fulfill the whole law. This seems to mean that they are to live in ways that embody what the law's commands convey, but to do it in ways that do not require Gentiles to become Jews. So while circumcision sets Jews apart as those dedicated to God and as members of the covenant with God, church members must embody being set apart and being in covenant in ways that are appropriate to who Gentiles are as well. This often requires sophisticated analysis of where they find themselves. Paul demands significant theological reflections from his churches. It is no wonder that he thinks they often needed to rethink the decisions they have reached.

Even as Paul argues that Gentiles must not observe the law as Jews do, he assumes and reinforces the connections between all believers (Jews and Gentiles) and Jewish heritage. Particularly, he argues that there is direct continuity between what God has done in Christ and what God promised Abraham. This continuity is vital for Paul. It is the God of Israel who acts through Christ to bring salvation and initiate the end times. The God of Jesus and of Paul is the God of Moses and Judaism; and the way God acts in Christ is consistent with and a continuation of what God had done with Abraham and Moses.

Finally, Paul's argument here reveals that the eschatological community, the church, is a community in which marks of status that the world recognizes do not bestow status. The baptismal liturgy quoted in 3:26-28 proclaims that differences of sex, ethnicity, and social status are inconsequential in the church. "In Christ" all take on the identity of Christ and so have equal value. This is not an imposition of sameness, but a leveling of the value placed on each person. Slaves are still slaves and women are still women, but their value is the same as those who are usually considered superior (owners and men). And Gentiles are still Gentiles and Jews are still Jews. Life in the eschatological church, then, demands a reorientation of the values by which a person lives and evaluates others. Paul's use of this liturgy here and in 1 Corinthians 7 suggests that his churches know it because he can use it to support his argument. Thus, it is a constant in his theology and his theologizing, that is, his use of his beliefs to interpret life and the world.

Suggested Reading

Charles B. Cousar. *Galatians*. Interpretation. Louisville: Westminster, 2012 (reprint of 1982 edition).

Martinus DeBoer. *Galatians: A Commentary.* New Testament Library. Louisville: Westminster John Knox, 2011.

L. Ann Jervis. *Galatians*. New International Biblical Commentary. Peabody, MA: Hendrickson, 1999.

Mark D. Nanos. *The Galatians Debate: Contemporary Issues in Rhetorical and Historical Interpretation*. Peabody, MA: Hendrickson, 2002.

Sam K. Williams. *Galatians*. Abingdon New Testament Commentary. Nashville: Abingdon, 1997.

Chapter 9

ROMANS

———— ⟨Ɔ∾᷁Ƈ⟩ ————

The Revelation of the Righteousness of God: Paul Introduces
Himself and His Gospel to a Church

Romans has often been considered Paul's most important letter. Not only is it the longest, but it has been seen as the letter that more objectively sets out his beliefs because he is not responding to a specific situation. While it is true that Paul gives a more methodical account of how some of his beliefs fit together, Romans is by no means an objective account of his teaching. Paul is, in fact, responding to a situation; it is different from the situations he responds to in other letters, but the situation still shapes significantly the way Paul presents himself and his gospel.

Three things shape the content of Romans. The first is Paul's desire to represent all Gentile believers when he delivers the Collection for Jerusalem. What is often called Paul's third missionary journey is really his travel to revisit churches he had already founded. Besides renewing relations and offering any instruction they may need, Paul took up financial contributions for the church in Judea on this trip. Members of the Jerusalem church had fallen on hard times, at least in part because of a famine. Paul sees this gift from his churches as a way to maintain unity between his predominantly Gentiles churches and the predominantly Jewish churches of Judea. We have already discussed how the success of the Gentile mission had led to difficult relations as the church rethought its identity in light of the influx of Gentiles (chapter 4).

Paul intends this gift to demonstrate to the predominantly Jewish churches that his predominantly Gentile churches know they owe a spiritual debt to the mother church (Rom 15:25-31). To accomplish this, he wants to represent all predominantly Gentile churches. Thus he wants to claim the Roman church among those he represents. The problem is that he that he did not found that church and has never been there. So with this letter he wants to convince the Roman church to recognize him as the apostle to all the Gentiles, including them (15:18-20). If they accept that understanding of Paul's ministry, he will be able to say that he represents all Gentile believers when he arrives in Jerusalem.

Paul's second purpose in writing Romans is to prepare the recipients for his arrival. He tells them that he has accomplished his work in the areas of Asia Minor (today's Turkey) and Greece, and so is ready to go to a new area. He intends to begin a new mission in Spain after he delivers the Collection to Jerusalem (15:22-25). He hopes the Roman church will help him on his way. He wants them to support his mission, probably financially but perhaps also by sending companions. Some speculate that he may not have been as fluent in Latin as he was in Greek. If that is the case, he may have wanted help communicating in the western part of the Empire.

The third purpose of this letter is to address some conflict between the Jewish and Gentile members of the church. The Roman church was not started by an apostle. It probably came into existence when some believers moved to Rome. It began as a predominantly Jewish church, but also attracted Gentiles. At some point the Gentiles became the predominant population in the church. Most interpreters think that the Edict of Claudius (c. 49) required many Jews to leave Rome, including most or all of those in the church. This meant that only Gentile members remained. When the Jewish believers began to return to Rome after the death of Claudius in 54, they did not receive as warm a welcome as they thought they should. As founding members, they expected to be recognized as leaders. But the Gentile members had recognized new leaders and perhaps had adopted some new practices.

Some interpreters contend that there was no Edict of Claudius since its existence relies on so few sources—and they are ambiguous. Even if there was no expulsion of a large number of Jews from Rome, Romans reveals significant tension between Jewish and Gentile members of this church. And in this case, it seems to flow in the opposite direction from that in Galatians. Rather than Jewish members urging Gentiles to be circumcised, in Rome it seems that the Gentile members are not pleased with Jews who continue their full association with the synagogue and expect those practices to be honored in the church. So Paul must argue for the legitimacy and even priority of Jews in the church.

Romans is written near the end of Paul's ministry. He writes it in about 58, just before leaving for Jerusalem, where he is arrested. If Philippians is written from Rome, it is the only extant letter that Paul certainly wrote after Romans. (It is possible that Philemon was written from Rome, so it may also be later.)

The whole of Romans addresses all three of the concerns named above, in part because they are related. Identifying himself as the apostle to the Gentiles helps Paul claim the Roman church and ask for their help in his mission, even as it positions him to defend the priority of Jews in the church.

Practical Problems and Responses

More than in other letters, Paul builds a cumulative argument in Romans. In 1 Corinthians, the first four chapters constitute a cumulative argument that lays the basis for his instructions that follow. But beginning in chapter 5, Paul addresses a series of issues the Corinthians have raised. In Romans, Paul develops a single line of argumentation through at least chapter 13. This does not mean it is a more objective argument, but it does remain more systematic in some ways. We will trace that argument to see how Paul presents his gospel to these believers he has never met, but who have heard about him—including having heard some things that he wants to deny.

The central themes of Romans appear in 1:16-17. In these verses Paul asserts that the gospel he proclaims is that God saves all people who have faith, even as Jews retain a priority. This gospel reveals the "righteousness of God." Paul intends "the righteousness of God" to include the many aspects of God's character that come to expression in the gospel. The prominent characteristics that emerge in Romans are God's holiness, faithfulness, justice, love, and mercy.

Paul says these aspects of God's character are revealed "through faith for faith." This phrase has been the subject of much discussion, in part because of the debates over the meaning of the term *faith* (*pistis*) in Romans. Among the things the Greek term *pistis* can mean are "faith" (largely a synonym of belief), "trust," "faithfulness," "trustworthiness." The debate about the meaning of *pistis* has centered on the phrase, "*pistis* of (Jesus) Christ" (e.g., in 3:22).

Translations usually render the phrase, "faith in Jesus Christ," but the footnote of the NRSV gives the alternative of "faith of Jesus Christ." The footnote translation suggests that Paul is referring to the faithfulness of Jesus, that is, to his obedience to the mission God had set out for him. If that is correct, then the phrase "through faith for faith" in 1:17 could mean that God's righteousness is seen "through faithfulness for faithfulness;" that it is seen in the faithfulness of Christ and that it, in turn, creates faithfulness in others. That understanding seems to fit the whole of what follows in Romans.

Paul begins introducing himself and his gospel by arguing that all people need the gospel because all people are guilty of things that deserve condemnation. Gentiles are guilty because they violate their own consciences. Jews have the advantage of possessing God's law, but are guilty because they violate it. Thus all people need the gospel (1:18–3:20). The gospel message of forgiveness through Christ is God's response to this human predicament. This message that Paul proclaims is also consistent with who God is known to be in scripture; it preserves the justice and holiness of God while also showing God to be loving and merciful (3:21-26). This gospel saves Gentiles without having them commit to the Mosaic covenant. Although this seems surprising since this covenant had been the way God's people had expressed their relationship with God, Paul argues that Abraham's relationship with God before he was circumcised affirms this element of his teaching (3:27–4:25).

In chapter 5, Paul shifts the image of how the gospel works from the law court (with guilty and not guilty verdicts as the concern) to that of personal relationship. He argues that all humans have positioned themselves as enemies of God by opposing God's will for the world. God responds in Christ by offering forgiveness and a renewed relationship (5:1-11).

But the problem the gospel addresses is deeper than specific acts that individuals commit. Paul envisions the sin of Adam as an act that had far-reaching effects. It introduced death into the world and submitted the world to the rule of powers that oppose God. Those who come after Adam have no choice but to be born into a world that requires them to conform to social, political, and economic structures that reflect the will of evil powers rather than God's will. Thus, all are trapped under the reign of sin and death. Paul says that God responds to this circumstance by sending Christ, whose obedience and death inaugurates a new era that frees people from the powers of evil, if they will only accept this gift (5:12-21).

Paul then pauses to answer possible misunderstandings. While humanity's sinfulness makes God's love all the more apparent, this is no excuse to continue doing evil. In fact, being freed from the rule of sin means that believers have been given life in the new realm. A believer enters that new realm through a baptism that puts the old self to death and raises him or her to a new existence, an existence in which obedience to God's will is the expected norm (6:1–7:6).

But Paul knows that the human struggle to do good is not resolved as easily as telling people that they have a new life. He knows that even while he tries to do good, he does what he should not. A part of him wants to do good but another part keeps doing wrong (7:7-25). In the end, he throws himself and all who want to live for God on God's mercy. Paul interprets the believer's experience of the Spirit as the promise that God will complete the task of bringing believers fully into God's presence at Christ's Second Coming (8:1-38).

All of this assurance of salvation is meaningful only if God is trustworthy. Some Gentile members of the Roman church seem to question whether the election of Israel is still valid. Perhaps they see their own relationship with God, which is maintained without participation in the Mosaic covenant, as proof that God has severed the special relationship with Israel. Paul devotes chapters 9–11 to confirming two propositions: (1) Israel's election is irrevocable, and (2) all salvation is in Christ. These stand in significant tension because the majority of Jews had not come to faith in Christ. Paul must affirm both of these propositions because the faithfulness of God is at stake. If God simply drops the relationship with Israel, then believers in Christ cannot be confident that God will not come up with something new and drop them. In the end, Paul is not sure how these two things fit together, but he knows they must both be true. So he ends this crucial section with a doxology that praises the inscrutable wisdom of God; only that wisdom can hold these truths together.

Many interpreters identify this discussion of the place of Israel as the climax of the argument of Romans. That is, all the explications of the need for the gospel and of the images for how it functions have had in view the affirmations of Israel's election and of God's faithfulness. Paul even sets his discussion of his apostleship in the context of God's faithfulness to Israel. This argument both affirms Paul's work as apostle to the Gentiles and assures Jewish believers that he has not abandoned faith in Israel's God, law, or election. In the course of his argument in chapters 3–8, Paul repeatedly defends the goodness and importance of the law as a means of revelation, even while maintaining that Gentiles do not submit to those commands that are marks of being in the Mosaic covenant. Chapters 9–11 add a defense of Israel's election. Thus, Paul argues, the conversion of Gentiles and God's commitment to Israel's salvation are compatible. Further, affirming both shows that God loves all people while being faithful to Israel.

Chapters 12–13 explicate the life that Paul says the gospel grants and demands. The proper response to receiving all the gifts Paul has enumerated in chapters 3–11 is that the recipients devote themselves wholly to God. Paul repeats a number of themes found in earlier letters: Believers should not think too highly of themselves; they should see the church as a body with parts that have different functions; and they must recognize love as a central Christian virtue. Paul reiterates that Gentiles fulfill the law by loving even though they do not observe those parts that are intended only for Jews. Thus, he again affirms the continuing importance of the law. These instructions are not just an addendum that show what believers should do as the consequence of accepting God's gifts. As he has said throughout the letter, the demand for ethical living is a part of God's gift. Living as God wants enriches existence as the believer is drawn into fuller participation in the new life given in Christ.

Paul has already spoken of these matters in earlier parts of the letter. In chapter 6, he contends that at baptism believers are given new life, new life that must be embodied by putting sin out of their lives. In chapter 8, he reminds them that having the presence of God in their lives must be manifested by living in accord with the Spirit. So there is an intimate and inseparable connection between what believers receive through Christ and how they live their lives because the new life is part of what they are given.

Chapters 14–15 address specific issues that are troubling the Roman church. These involve food restrictions and the observance of holy days. Some church members in Rome abide by food restrictions they think all believers should follow. Paul says that some members eat only vegetables and pass judgment against those who eat meat, while others eat meat and look down on those who eat only vegetables (14:1-4). It is difficult to tell why some members have given up eating meat. Given that there are also questions about holy days, the dispute may involve how the church relates to the Mosaic instructions about food and holy days. However, the law does not demand that people be vegetarians. So unless Paul is exaggerating to make his point, more than the law is involved. Yet the debate about holy days most likely does involve the law because Paul would not think that celebrating pagan holy days is compatible with faith in Christ.

Paul's central response is that such matters should not divide the church. Rather each person should follow her or his conscience in these matters. Each faces God's judgment, and that should be enough to discern which of the options conforms to God's will for him or her (14:1-6). This does not mean that a person can decide that anything (e.g., robbery or adultery) is permissible. But there is a category of decisions about behavior in which a decision to abstain or partake is a personal one. But there are two caveats.

The first restriction is that what the person does must be in accord with his or her own conscience. For example, to decide to eat meat when you think it is wrong is a sin. This is not because eating meat is wrong (Paul says eating meat is not wrong), but because you act in ways *you think* are wrong. That makes you guilty before God because it is a breach of faithfulness to what you believe God wants you to do (14:20-23). So failure to follow one's own conscience in these matters constitutes a failure to live for God.

Given what we have seen in other letters, it is not surprising that Paul adds an element beyond an individualistic resolution to these issues. The second consideration is the effect your decision has on the rest of the church. Believers are not permitted to behave in ways that will cause others to violate their consciences. So they must not show disapproval of the person who abstains and they must not exercise their freedom in a way that leads others to be unfaithful to what they think God wants (14:13-20).

In addition to these specific issues, the letter addresses the broader question of the place of the law. Paul made strong statements about what the law cannot do in Galatians. Perhaps this and other claims he had made about the law in disputes with those who want Gentiles to be circumcised and observe the law in the way the Jewish community observed it had led some to assert that Paul did not value the law. They may even suggest that Paul contends that receiving grace means that believers can sin as much as they want (Rom 3:7-8). Throughout Romans, Paul argues that the law is important for Christians and that it reveals the will of God, even as it is not a means of salvation. Besides asserting that the law and the prophets testify to his gospel (3:21), he insists that the gospel does not overthrow the law (3:31). He says that the law is a good thing; it is holy and just and good (7:12; see also 7:7, 13). So he responds to the charge that he does not value the law by affirming that it has continuing functions.

Watching Paul Work

Throughout Romans, Paul uses a number of rhetorical or argumentative devices to help him persuade these readers about who he is, what he teaches, why they should support him, and how they should resolve problems within their churches. One prominent tool in the first chapters of the letter is diatribe. Whether Paul follows the detailed rules for this literary device or not, he uses its basic form. In diatribe the speaker or writer imagines an antagonist raising problems and objections at various points in an argument. A clear example is 3:7. After arguing that all have sinned and that human sin makes the faithfulness of God even more obvious, the objector says, "If it makes God look good, why not sin all the more?" (3:5-8, paraphrased). When his unseen interlocutor asks such questions, it allows Paul to turn the conversation in the direction he wants it to go. So while these questions appear as objections, Paul frames them so that he gets to address the next issue he thinks is important.

As he had in Galatians, Paul also uses Abraham as an example of the way God works among God's people. As the original recipient of the promise, Abraham is the pattern for those who come after him. In Romans 4, Abraham's relationship with God is secured by trusting God. That attitude of trust becomes the authoritative pattern for believers in Christ. At the same time, Paul uses Abraham to argue that Gentiles must not submit to circumcision because in the Genesis story Abraham is declared righteous before he is circumcised. Abraham is more than a revered ancient model, he is also the beginning point of God's work that comes to fullness in Christ. While there are significant differences in the ways Paul uses Abraham in Romans and Galatians, in both letters Abraham is the authoritative pattern that shows how God lives in relationship with people.

Adam also plays an important role in Romans. Rather than being a paradigm for how believers relate to God, he serves as a "type" for Christ. That is, his action is paralleled, and in some ways repeated, in Christ. In this role, Adam is more than a historical figure, he sets a pattern for the way things are. Adam is a type because his actions affected all people. Christ is the antitype, the repeater of the pattern, because his actions affected all. Since readers accept the idea that Adam's action (his sin) brought death to all, it makes sense to say that Christ's action can bring life to all. The Adam type shows that the church's claim that Christ changed things for all people is not without parallel and in fact is supported by an ancient precedent.

110

Paul also uses scripture as an authority in Romans, particularly in chapters 3–4 and 9–11. These important sections concern the place of Jews within God's plan. In chapters 3–4, Paul contends that Jews need the gospel as much as Gentiles and that their ancestor validates his gospel. In chapters 9–11, he argues that God remains faithful to Israel so that their election means that they retain a priority in the gospel. Using scripture allows him to present arguments that draw on texts that Jews (especially, but also believing Gentiles) regard as authoritative.

Paul draws on a different type of authority in chapter 16. Although some argue that chapter 16 was added at a later time, most interpreters see it as an original part of Romans. If it is original, Paul greets more people here than in any other letter—and he has never visited this church. Greeting all these people bolsters his position in relation to the Roman church. He has never been there, but he has good relations with many of its leaders. Their familiarity with him grants him credibility; they can vouch for his reliability and authenticity. Thus, the Roman church is more likely to accept his advice and more likely to accept him as the apostle of their church.

When Paul addresses the problem of whether food restrictions and certain holy days should be observed, he offers three different arguments. The first is that each person is primarily responsible to God. Every believer belongs to God and so judgment should be left to God when it comes to matters like food. This assertion cuts two ways: It frees the believer from the evaluation of other believers (14:4), but it makes them responsible to God (14:4, 10, 12, 22). So believers do not face the judgment of one another, but they do face God's judgment.

As we noted above, despite this individualistic-sounding response, Paul is concerned about the health of the community. Believers must not behave in ways that cause others to sin. He supports this assertion by repeating some of the central arguments of 1 Corinthians. Believers must not cause another to sin because fellow believers are so valuable that Christ died for them (14:15). When they welcome the more scrupulous person, they are following Christ's example of putting the other's good ahead of their own (15:1-4). While he does not use the phrase, this points them to what he calls the "word of the cross" in 1 Corinthians. Such an evaluation of the other and following such an example leads each person to seek peace rather than engage in arguments about nonessential matters.

The third argument for having different people live by different rules about food and holy days is that all of one's life should be lived as an act of faith. In everything a person does, he or she lives for Christ (14:7-9). He goes so far as to say that the person who violates his own conscience sins because he is violating his faith; he is doing something he believes is wrong (14:23).

What We Learn about Paul

As Paul presents his gospel and his apostleship in Romans, he looks at the human problem from a number of perspectives and shows how the gospel is God's gracious response to each level of viewing what separates people from God and from one another. These different angles give us glimpses of important elements of Paul's theology. He envisions each person as responsible for her or his own behavior. Thus, violating God's will brings genuine guilt. But his eschatology also informs his understanding of the situation in which humans find themselves. Because the cosmos is controlled by the powers of sin and death (the names given the evil that governs the cosmos), humans are trapped and unable to free themselves from domination that demands that a person engages in sin. But the problem is even deeper; sin lives within each person.

Each time Paul presents an analysis of the human condition, he explains the way the gospel addresses it. For Paul the work of Christ allows God to express love and mercy by forgiving, reconciling, and rescuing humanity while God also maintains the characteristics of holiness and justice. The human need for the gospel and the grace extended in the eschatological gospel to Jews and Gentiles make the gospel a demonstration of the righteousness of God. Romans shows that Paul thinks that coherence in his theology is important. The understandings of both the human condition and God's responses also demonstrate why both Jews and Gentiles need his gospel. Thus, these presentations of the gospel support his commission as apostle to the Gentiles.

Many of the arguments Paul uses in chapters 14–15 he had used in 1 Corinthians and will use in Philippians. He speaks of fellow believers as people for whom Christ died, he contends that people should act in the best interest of others rather than their own, and he asserts that food in itself cannot defile. Because he identifies his instructions about these matters as manifestations of love (see Rom 13:8-10; 1 Cor 13), love appears as central theme in the ways Paul guides behavior in his churches.

The shape of the argument in Romans suggests that Paul's theology consists of working through various problems and analyses of the state of things in light of who he knows God to be through his Jewish faith and through his understanding of how God has acted in Christ. It is the God of Israel whose righteousness is revealed in the gospel.

Suggested Reading

David L. Bartlett. *Romans*. Westminster Bible Companion. Louisville: Westminster John Knox, 1995.

C. E. B. Cranfield. *Romans: A Shorter Commentary*. Grand Rapids: Eerdmans, 1985.

A. Andrew Das. *Solving the Romans Debate*. Minneapolis: Fortress, 2007.

Karl P. Donfried. *The Romans Debate*. 2nd ed. Grand Rapids: Baker Academic, 1991.

Joseph A. Fitzmyer. *Romans : A New Translation with Introduction and Commentary*. Anchor Bible. New York: Doubleday, 1993.

Leander E. Keck. *Romans*. Abingdon New Testament Commentary. Nashville: Abingdon, 2005.

Jerry L. Sumney, editor. *Reading Paul's Letter to the Romans*. Resources for Biblical Study. Atlanta: SBL Press, 2012.

N. T. Wright. *Paul and the Faithfulness of God*. Minneapolis: Fortress, 2014.

Chapter 10

PHILIPPIANS AND PHILEMON

Consider Others Better Than Yourself

The first church Paul established in Europe was in Philippi (4:15-16; see also Acts 16:1-15). When he arrived in Macedonia, the northern region of Greece, this is the first city in which he set up a mission. Paul maintained good relations with this church throughout his life, accepting financial support from them even while he refused it from the Corinthians.

Paul wrote this letter when he was in prison, but we cannot be sure when and where he was in prison. Although Paul was in prison often (2 Cor 11:23), most interpreters see three options for where Paul was when he wrote Philippians: Ephesus, Caesarea, and Rome. While Ephesus continues to have a great deal of support, most recent commentators think Paul wrote this letter from Rome. If this is correct, it means that Philippians is Paul's last letter, being written perhaps in 60–63. But determining the date for its writing does not significantly affect our understanding of this letter because the issues it addresses are unrelated to which imprisonment Paul is enduring. We will deal with the short letter of Philemon in this chapter because it may well have been written at about the same time and under the same circumstances.

The seemingly abrupt change in topic at 3:1 and the delay in thanking the recipients for a gift (4:10-20) has led some interpreters to find fragments of three letters combined in canonical Philippians. The continuity in rhetorical flow, however, suggests that it is more likely a single letter.

Practical Problems and Responses

Philippians is known as a letter of joy. Paul talks more about rejoicing in this letter than in any other, but he must also address a serious problem. Paul does not explicitly name the central issue until 4:2. There is dissention within the community that is growing from a dispute between two well-known leaders, Euodia and Syntyche. Paul seldom singles out by name people who are causing trouble, but he does here. These leaders had served with Paul in his mission work and so he knows them well. The way Paul deals with them shows both his concern for the unity of the church and his respect for these leaders' work in the church. This makes it all the more important to recognize that they are both women. Paul's dealings with them and his recognition of their leadership are clear evidence that Paul affirms the leadership of women in his churches.

Once we know that the problem is a dispute between leaders, the argument of most of the rest of the letter makes excellent sense. It is focused on resolving the dispute. But the seemingly sudden turn to talk about teachers who demand that Gentiles be circumcised at 3:1 appears out of place. Although some interpreters have suggested that such teachers are present in Philippi, this brief rejection of them is probably a warning about their possible arrival. (We will discuss an additional function of Paul's mention of these teachers below.)

This church is also being troubled by opposition from outside (1:28). When Paul mentions his own imprisonment, he gives it an unexpected interpretation. Everyone assumed that prison brought shame and signaled defeat. Having leaders of your group imprisoned would be seen as a setback, as evidence that something was seriously wrong. But Paul says his imprisonment has advanced the gospel! Not only has it spread the message in places it would not have reached otherwise but that result has also emboldened other believers to share the gospel with outsiders (1:12-14).

This line of interpretation helps the Philippians think about Paul, but it serves a second important purpose. It helps them interpret their own experience of persecution. In 1:27-30, Paul acknowledges that the Philippians are enduring persecution. This persecution probably took the form of suffering social and economic disadvantages because of their membership in the church. He encourages them to stand firm despite this opposition by interpreting their steadfastness as evidence of their salvation and of the condemnation of those who trouble them. Then he explicitly connects their suffering and his. So if his suffering can advance the gospel, so can theirs. He both identifies himself with their suffering and assures them that it can have a good result.

In addition to addressing these problems, Paul thanks the Philippians for the financial support they have just sent him. In his thank-you, he interprets their gift so that they see it as more than a part of their relationship with him. He uses the language of worship to describe this gift. In language taken from Leviticus (e.g., 1:9, 13, 17; 2:12), he interprets their support of his mission as a sacrificial offering to God that is on a par with what is sacrificed in the temple. Their support of his mission, then, is more than a proper response to the good things he brought them; it is a genuine act of worship. So their participation in his ministry is a way to honor God.

The dispute between Euodia and Syntyche is a dominant issue, but not the only one discussed. Even though it is the pressing issue, Paul gives no hint about the subject of the dispute. It seems not to matter. The effect it is having on life within the church is more important. Their dispute at least had the potential to divide and so to weaken the church. Paul's response focuses on the need for harmony within the church and on how the gospel calls church members to treat one another in the midst of disagreements.

Watching Paul Work

One of the ways Paul commonly encourages his readers to listen is to compliment them. He does this in the introductory thanksgivings of most of his letters. He compliments the Philippians by telling them that he is confident that God is working in them. He also reminds them of their mutual love and their history of good relations (1:6-7; see also 1:27-30). Throughout the letter, he also develops his ethos as one who cares for them. In fact, he loves them so much he is willing to suffer (1:25-26) or even to die for them (2:17-18). He develops this ethos and elicits emotion by telling them of his unjust treatment (1:15-18). Rhetoricians noted that the image of a good person suffering unjustly engendered pity and made audiences receptive (Quintillian 2.34; Aristotle, *Rhet* 2.8.8, 16).

Paul uses repetition to dramatize and emphasize the need for unity. He uses this tool in 2:1-2. In verse 1, he begins a sentence that sets out a condition ("If then there is any...") and then repeats and restates the condition four times before he gives the second part of the sentence. This was sure to get their attention. His completion of the sentence is a series of phrases that repeat the words *same* or *one*. Similarly, as he concludes his exhortations in 4:8-9, he writes a series of identical phrases ("whatever is..."). These virtues exemplify what the Philippians have been taught and shown about how to live together as the church.

As he does in other letters, Paul also cites an authority to convince the Philippians to follow his instructions. The material in 2:6-11 is often identified as an early Christian hymn. Its meter and heightened style show that it is not common prose. While it may not be precisely a hymn, it is a liturgical piece that the Philippians know. Its account of the descent, incarnation, death, and resurrection of Christ serve as a central support for instructions about proper conduct within the community. Paul's initial direct response to the dispute between Euodia and Syntyche and the dissention in the church comes in 2:3-5. All members are to consider others better than themselves and to put the good of others above their own good. They will be able to do this when they adopt the mind-set of Christ that is seen in the liturgy Paul quotes in verses 6-11.

The most important and pervasive type of argument in Philippians is the presentation of examples that the Philippians are to imitate. Paul opens the letter describing his willingness to endure suffering for them, and he ends his exhortations in 4:9 telling them to adopt the manner of life they have seen in him. The solution he gives to the dispute in the church is for everyone to imitate the examples he mentions. The exemplar that all the other examples imitate is Christ as he is seen in the liturgy. He gave up significant position and power for the benefit of others. Without saying it directly, Paul has already presented himself as someone who follows this example: While he would prefer being with Christ, he continues to endure suffering for the Philippians' good (1:21-26).

Having introduced the liturgy as the model for how to live in relation to one another, Paul interprets that exemplar as a summons to stop bickering and to get along with one another (2:12-15). As he gives this interpretation, he again introduces his care for the Philippians as an example of how they should live. He is willing to be sacrificed for their good—and they should rejoice that he has that attitude (2:17-18). So Paul follows the example of Christ, just as he wants them to follow it.

Paul next gives Timothy as another example of the same way of living.

In contrast to other people, Timothy puts the good of others—including the Philippians—ahead of his own good (2:20-21). The following paragraph gives Epaphroditus, a member of their church, as another example of someone who has adopted this way of living. He risked his life serving the rest of the church (2:25-30, esp. vv. 29-30).

The seemingly strange warning about those who want Gentile believers to accept circumcision may make more sense if we see use of example as Paul's pervasive strategy to convince the church and its leaders to stop arguing. The reference to those rejected teachers allows Paul to show again how he followed Christ's example. Paul had significant religious advantages before joining the church, but he gave them up. His willingness to resign those privileges resulted in two things: receiving the blessings of salvation in Christ and suffering. Paul is even an example of someone who has not fully been conformed to the prime exemplar, Christ (3:12-16). So even though the Philippians have failed to emulate Christ, they can renew their effort just as Paul constantly does.

Immediately following Paul's acknowledgment of striving to become like Christ, he renews the call for them to imitate him. But now he urges them to be fellow imitators (3:17). Paul and the Philippians are coimitators of Christ. At the same time, they should imitate others around them who adopt the pattern of life Paul has described. This exhortation demonstrates that Timothy and Epaphroditus were described earlier so that they could serve as examples of how the Philippians should live.

In 3:18, Paul explicitly identifies a bad example. Just as the Philippians should imitate Christ and others who exemplify his willingness to privilege the good of others, so are they to avoid acting like other people. They must not be like these "enemies of the cross," who delight in shame (3:18-19). They are the opposite of what the Philippians must be. This may explain why Paul mentions those who want Gentile believers circumcised; they serve as an example of what the readers must not be. They are evildoers who put confidence in the flesh. They are the alternative to following the example of Paul. Paul intentionally makes that alternative unattractive. Similarly, those who preach in order to cause Paul grief also serve as examples of what not to be (1:15-17). Paul says their motives are envy and rivalry. Perhaps this is a not-so-veiled comment about the root of the dissension at Philippi.

One final aspect of this imitation may be helpful to the Philippians. When Paul is persecuted it does not result in shame or defeat, even if he is executed

(1:19-20). The only shame would be in denying his faith. Furthermore, his suffering spreads the gospel rather than hinders it. In this acceptance of suffering combined with good being accomplished, Paul is again conforming to Christ's example. When Christ willingly accepted disadvantage, God exalted him. Paul has said that his being conformed to Christ will culminate in the resurrection (2:19-21). If the Philippians can see their suffering as an imitation of Christ and of Paul (1:30), then they may be able to envision that it accomplishes good rather than just inflicting shame and that it will culminate in resurrection.

The central theological claims on which Paul builds his argument in Philippians all relate to the incarnation, death, and exaltation of Christ. This narrative serves as the paradigm for Christian living. The liturgical material in 2:6-11 has been very influential in the development of doctrines of Christology, but Paul does not use it to develop a Christology. Paul is here interested solely in the pattern he sees: Christ accepted severe disadvantage at the incarnation, this commitment to privilege the good of others extended to a willingness to die for them, then God exalted him. That three-stage pattern is the foundation of and central support for the main purpose of this letter.

Paul makes his reason for quoting the liturgy explicit in 2:3-5. He says they are to adopt the pattern of thought and life seen in the story of the incarnation, passion, and exaltation of Christ. They will consider others better than themselves and put the good of others above their own good. Thus, the fundamental function of the dominant theological element of the text is to support an ethical exhortation. All of the other examples given in the text are evaluated by how well they conform to the pattern seen in Christ. All who conform to vital elements of the pattern serve as examples to emulate; all who fail to conform are illustrations of what to avoid. The only modification appears when Paul says he is still struggling to conform fully. But even here his desire and effort to conform serves as the desirable model.

While the predominant aspect of the model is giving up privilege for the good of others, God's response to that manner of life is also important. As God exalted Christ, so those who adopt Christ's manner of life will be raised to life with God. Paul expects this for himself (1:20-24) and for other believers (1:28-30). Just as the exaltation of Christ was an act of God, so is the resurrection of believers. After mentioning how he labors to shape his life to be like Christ, the prototype, he affirms that the resurrection, that final conformity to Christ, is an act of God (3:20-21). Even as he presses the

Philippians to adopt the proper manner of life, he says that both the power and the desire to assume it come from God (2:12-13). So God enables God's people to live in accord with the exemplar seen in the descent, incarnation, death, and exaltation of Christ.

Belief in the judgment plays a substantive role in the argument of the letter as well. The certainty of judgment on the wicked is important for a church enduring persecution. It promises vindication of their faithfulness and of the faithfulness of God's love and justice. So their persecutors face condemnation that is already signaled in their conduct (1:28). The fate of those "enemies of the cross" (whoever they are) is destruction (3:18-19). But the judgment is not only for those enemies. Paul tells the Philippians they need to "work out your own salvation with fear and trembling" (2:12). This expression does not mean they must earn their place with God; rather, immediately following the liturgy about Christ, it tells them that their conduct must embody the salvation they have been given. That embodiment is a required part of having received God's grace. This new way of life distinguishes them from the evil people around them and shows that they are God's children (2:14-15). So, learning to live in conformity with the exemplar in the liturgy is a necessity of the believer's life.

What We Learn about Paul

As has been the case in several letters, some of what we learn about Paul and his thought emerges incidentally rather than being a significant part of the way he makes his argument. In Philippians we see elements of his Christology that he does not argue for, but assumes. As he cites the liturgical material in 2:6-11, we see that his churches believe in and recite a narrative of Christ's descent, incarnation, death, and exaltation. Paul's Christology here includes the preexistence of Christ and an exaltation that makes him the highest being that all will eventually acknowledge. This Christology, in turn, includes belief in an eschatological scenario that envisions the defeat and subjection of all powers of evil. This decisive moment includes the judgment of those who oppose the purposes of God and of those in the church. Here again Paul's Christology and eschatology are necessarily intertwined.

Paul's emphasis on Christology in Philippians still acknowledges that God is the primary actor in salvation, even in the liturgy's narrative. Christ is obedient to God (2:8) and God is the one who exalts Christ (2:9). Christ is

God's agent and the one through whom God works, but remains subordinate to God. Even the final recognition of Christ's lordship has the goal of bringing honor to God (2:11). Further, the righteousness produced through Christ and recognized at judgment has as its final goal bringing honor and praise to God (1:3, 10-11). So Paul's theology remains theocentric.

Paul does not insist that the church believe what the liturgy of 2:6-11 proclaims; he just assumes they all do believe it. So he can use these beliefs to addresses the problem of division. This christological narrative provides a fundamental exemplar for ethics. That exemplar is again very similar to what Paul calls the "word of the cross" in 1 Corinthians 1–4. There, the willingness of Christ to die for the good of others is the model for Christian spirituality and communal life. In Philippians, Paul expresses the same basic theological idea in a new form. His Christology has not changed, but how he constructs his argument has. Perhaps the difficulties at Corinth led him to try the new rhetorical strategy of giving more stress to other examples of the proper pattern of life in Philippians.

Philippians continues to demonstrate the centrality of the community in Paul's thought. What is good for the church is more important that whatever the Philippian leaders are arguing about. The good of the church takes precedence over the good of the individual in all of the letter's good examples. Christ, Paul, Timothy, and Epaphroditus all accept disadvantage for the good of the church. This pattern expresses the important connections between Paul's ethics, ecclesiology, and Christology. His understanding of Christ shapes those other aspects of his theology.

Some find the call to imitation oppressive, as a demand for rigid conformity. If the criticism is that Paul wants the Philippians to behave in a particular way and to stop behaving in others, then it is warranted. He certainly wants to correct their behavior and uses powerful means to do so. If he had not wanted to convince others, he would not have bothered to write. But calling for imitation does not demand narrow and rigid uniformity. Following Paul's example does not mean the Philippians need to seek imprisonment. It does mean that acceptable behavior is that which reflects the exemplar seen in the liturgy of 2:6-11.

The ideas of considering others more important than ourselves and of putting the good of others first have also been criticized as oppressive. There are many examples where women have been told to remain in abusive situations to put the good of others first. Such uses of this exemplar are extreme misuses of it. They fail to see a vital part of the pattern. That crucial element is that this pattern expects the one who has privilege and power to give it up. Imitating Christ's acts calls those with power to give it up. Even in the context of Philippians, those who most directly need to adopt this mode of life are leaders. With that said, the behavior Paul advocates was then and remains very countercultural.

Philemon

This shortest letter in the Pauline corpus is also the only undisputed letter written primarily to an individual rather than to a church. Even though really to Philemon, the church of which he is a member is also addressed in the greeting. The letter concerns a single issue, the return of Onesimus, Philemon's slave.

Nearly everything about the situation remains obscure. It is not clear why Onesimus is with Paul. Some think he had run away from perhaps an abusive master (Philemon), others that he had gone to Paul to appeal for help in some dispute with his master. Paul is in prison, but we cannot be sure where. Traditionally, Rome was identified as the place of imprisonment, but it is so far from Colossae (where Philemon lives) that this seems unlikely. Other known imprisonments of Paul have their difficulties too. But the letter is probably written late in his career because Paul identifies himself as an old man (9). Neither is it clear what Paul wants Philemon to do. Some think Paul suggests that Philemon free his slave, others that he take Onesimus back under new conditions since the slave is now a church member (15-16), and still others that Paul wants Philemon to send Onesimus to serve him.

Practical Problem and Solution

This much is clear: The slave and master are estranged. Paul says Onesimus (whose name means "useful") formerly was useless to Philemon, but now is useful. Further, Paul says that if Onesimus owes Philemon anything Paul will repay it (18-19).

The lack of clarity in what Paul requests shows that this work does not set out Paul's position on slavery. The early church did not attempt to change the structures of the Roman social order, perhaps because they envisioned the Second Coming as imminent or perhaps because they knew that their small movement could not withstand the persecution that would have followed an attempt to eradicate slavery. The Qumran community did oppose slavery, but they withdrew from the economic and social life of the world around them. The church remained in the city. Given that environment, any movement to emancipate slaves, even those owned by church members, would have been seen as an act of insurrection. What Paul does say (that Onesimus is now a brother) undermines slavery, but he does not explicitly reject the institution.

Paul does call for the restoration of Onesimus without him suffering any repercussions for his actions, whatever they may have been. Paul adds that he gives thanks for the love Philemon has shown to fellow believers (4-7). Paul makes his appeal for Onesimus on the basis of that feature of Philemon's character (8). This thanksgiving and appeal also confirm that love was recognized as a central virtue in Paul's churches.

Paul also bases his appeal on the relationship he has with Philemon. Apparently, Philemon was converted by Paul or by Paul's mission partners because Paul says that Philemon owes him his very self. Thus, complying with this request is simply a partial repayment of that debt. It is not just the relationship between these two that is at stake. By including the church in the greeting, this affair becomes public knowledge and an ecclesial matter. Thus, how Philemon responds will affect his relationship with others in his church who also have a relationship with Paul.

Finally, there is an implicit threat in the closing verses of the letter. Paul asks Philemon to prepare a room for him because he is planning to visit. By mentioning this, Paul intimates that he will be there to see how Philemon has responded to his appeal.

Watching Paul Work

On some levels, the argument in this letter is very tactful; on others it is rather pointed. Paul makes few explicit or specific requests, but his argumentation leaves no room for Philemon to refuse his implied appeals. The dominant argument is based on pathos, emotion. This is particularly prominent in Paul's self-presentation. Rather than building an ethos that makes him reliable and authoritative, Paul presents himself as someone for whom one should feel pity. He does not introduce himself as an apostle in the greeting, but only as a prisoner. Then he appeals to Philemon as an old man and a prisoner (10). Being in prison was bad enough to evoke sympathy, but Paul suffers there in his old age. He is someone Philemon should support because he is in prison for the gospel (13). Because Onesimus is now Paul's "son," it would cause this old imprisoned man even more pain if something bad happened to him.

Paul also works from the assumed virtue of reciprocity. Paul has given Philemon more than he could ever repay, and now asks for something small in return. The cultural value of responding to gifts would have left Philemon no room to refuse. Paul mentions that Onesimus has taken Philemon's place in service to Paul, assuming that this was a proper response of Philemon to the gift Paul has given. Then Paul assures Philemon that his wants this response to be voluntary, so he returns Onesimus. The precise nature of the response may be voluntary, but culturally it is a nearly inescapable demand. This seems fairly clear in verses 19-20.

The expectation that Philemon will respond positively is not based solely on debt, but also on Philemon's character. The ethos that Paul sketches of Philemon makes him a loving person who expresses that love by helping fellow believers (4-7). Having remembered him in this complementary manner, Paul now calls on Philemon to live up to that portrayal of his character: He is to receive this new believer with the loving attitude for which he is known. To make certain that this element of his appeal is not missed, Paul comments that he is sure Philemon will do even more than he is asked.

What We Learn about Paul

Although Paul relies on pathos in other places in his letters, it is nowhere as dominant as it is in Philemon. Paul's request does not depend directly on any theological argumentation. It does assume that love is a cardinal virtue of the community and that believers recognize one another as siblings. By making a point of not exercising his apostolic authority, Paul's mention of these things make them a part of the grounding of the demand (8-9). An implicit grounding in his apostolic authority appears in the request that Philemon prepare for a visit from him. Beyond expecting that his apostolic office confers some authority, Paul shows he is willing to rely heavily on emotional appeals and on cultural conventions when they lead to proper conduct within the church.

So we learn nothing new about Paul's theology from this letter, but we do see another way that he worked within his churches. His theology of oneness in Christ produces a muted critique of the slavery system because his description of Onesimus's new identity (he is a brother) is incompatible with holding him as a slave. Perhaps expecting Philemon to reach that conclusion is an aspect of Paul saying that Philemon will do "more than I ask" (21).

Suggested Reading

John M. G. Barclay. *Colossians and Philemon*. T. & T. Clark Study Guides. New York: T. & T. Clark, 2001.

Charlie B. Cousar. *Philippians and Philemon*. New Testament Library. Louisville: Westminster John Knox, 2009.

Stephen Fowl. *Philippians*. Two Horizons New Testament Commentary. Grand Rapids: Eerdmans, 2005.

Larry J. Kreitzer, *Philemon*. Readings. Sheffield: Sheffield Phoenix Press, 2008.

Carolyn Osiek. *Philippians, Philemon*. Abingdon New Testament Commentaries. Nashville: Abingdon, 2000.

Todd D. Still. *Philippians and Philemon*. Smyth & Helwys Bible Commentary. Macon, GA: Smyth & Helwys, 2011.

Part III

THE DISPUTED LETTERS

Chapter 11

COLOSSIANS

---·❦·---

Forgiveness and Spirituality in Christ

Many scholars think that some letters in the Pauline corpus were not actually penned by Paul but were written in his name. A few think that some of these may have been written at his behest, but most contend that they were written after his death. When modern readers hear that a book was written in the name of a person without their permission, we think of forgeries. But ancient writers and readers often thought that writing in the name of a deceased person was a legitimate way of extending that person's influence and propagating his views. The practice of writing in the name of a person who had died was a widely used practice among philosophers and among apocalyptic writers. Some philosophers wrote texts in the names of long-dead predecessors. Some wrote letters purporting to be from Socrates more than 300 years after his death. Within Judaism, many apocalyptic writers wrote in the names of people who were characters in Genesis or who had been prophets or leaders during the return from the exile in Babylon. Even living people sometimes gave permission for people to write things in their name. In a letter to Atticus, Cicero says this: "To whomever you think right, please send letters in my name—you know my friends. If they look for my seal or handwriting, say that I have foregone these on account of the sentries" (11.2). This way of construing authorship is rather different from the ways we think about it today.

Writing in the name of dead but well-known people not only increased the writers' influence, it also lent credibility to the message of the real author. Writing in the name of Abraham, Enoch, or Ezra gave a text immediate authority. The same was true for writing in the name of earlier philosophers. The real authors thought they were saying what these deceased people would say if they were here now. These authors thought they were making the proper application of what was known of earlier venerable person to a new time. Later readers may think that the pseudonymous writer misrepresented the views of the claimed author, but these writers were often addressing their times and issues in the way the claimed author would have.

As we read these texts that claim to be written by Paul but probably were not, we can observe how they develop the teaching found in the undisputed letters. We can consider the ways they extend that teaching to address new situations. Some of the types of arguments we saw in Paul's authentic letters will remain the same, but these letters also produce new kinds of arguments. Some of the positions these letters take stand in significant tension with things found in Paul's letters. Perhaps the new situation demanded a different response or perhaps the author misunderstood Paul. In either case, the early church found enough consistency to attribute them all to Paul and to include them among its authoritative writings.

Colossians

Just more than half of critical scholars find Colossians to be pseudonymous. While there is nothing in the letter that Paul could not have said, it goes beyond what Paul does say in its interpretation of his suffering. In addition, Colossians has a section known as a household code. None of the undisputed letters have such a section, while at least two other of the disputed letters have them. It is the accumulation of these and other factors that lead many interpreters to think that Colossians was penned shortly after Paul's death.

Unlike most Pauline letters, Colossians purportedly addresses a church that Paul did not personally found. It falls within his sphere of influence because it was established by one of his coworkers, probably Epaphroditus (1:7-8; 2:1). The letter assumes that the real recipients (who were probably not in Colossae, because it was destroyed by an earthquake in 60–62) recognize Paul as an apostle and as authoritative for the church.

Practical Problems and Responses

The whole of Colossians addresses a single issue. Despite this, interpreters disagree about the nature of the teaching Colossians opposes. Many interpreters think that some are advocating that church members begin to worship angels who provide a path to spiritual experiences or might block access to God. They may also claim, as other religions in the region did, that worshiping these angels could bring healing of various illnesses. Some practices of Judaism also form a part of this teaching.

Other New Testament scholars, however, think that Colossians would more directly oppose worshiping other beings if these teachers advocated such worship. These interpreters understand the phrase "worship of angels" (2:18) to refer to the worship that angels perform (rather than worship offered to them), a parallel to talking about the "worship of the church." Such teachers argue that believers need to participate in the worship that angels offer to God. Access to this worship comes through visionary experiences in which a person sees the heavenly liturgy and participates in it with angels. These teachers claim that without this experience a person is not really saved and has not been forgiven of his or her sins. Thus, they question the salvation of those who have not accepted their teaching. Some practices of Judaism are incorporated as elements of a regimen designed to evoke mystical experiences. Colossians opposes this teaching because it does not see faith in the work of Christ as sufficient for salvation.

The forgiveness of sins is a central topic of Colossians. In the face of a teaching that says only those with extraordinary visionary experiences (or only those who go through angels) have received God's forgiveness, Colossians proclaims that forgiveness comes through identification with Christ. No other experiences are necessary. While Colossians uses many metaphors for salvation (no less than five in 1:12-13), the most important way it speaks of salvation is as forgiveness. Forgiveness is the climax of the list of metaphors in 1:12-13 and it is the point of the liturgical material in 1:15-20, as both the preceding and following verses make clear. There the exalted place of Christ assures believers that they are granted forgiveness and relationship with God through Christ.

The writer contends that believers receive forgiveness and relationship with God at baptism, not in some mystical experience. In 2:11-15, baptism is identified as the place believers are forgiven and where they become members of the new covenant. Metaphors associated with baptism appear throughout the letter. Believers have been raised with Christ (3:1), have stripped off their old selves (3:9), and have put on the clothing that identifies them with Christ (3:10, 14). These are well-known metaphors for what takes place in baptism. Thus, all that is being promised in the visionary experiences has already been given to those who have been baptized. So the other teaching is superfluous.

Colossians also directly addresses the demands the other teachers make. Most of the description of the elements of the other teaching appears in the polemical section of 2:8-23. Since this is a highly charged argumentative attack, we must be aware that the writer caricatures these demands. Still, we are able to see the kinds of things the other teachers require. They demand some food and holy day regulations, at least some of which (such as Sabbaths) come from Jewish practices (2:16-23). Their rules prohibit some types of food and involve some at least mildly ascetic withdrawal from some pleasures (2:21-23). In other first-century groups that value visionary experiences, prohibitions about food and other bodily pleasures (often including sexual abstinence) are expected components in a regime that leads to a visionary experience. So it seems probable that these regulations are in force on holy days as ways to bring about the desired visions.

Colossians rejects these regulations and the requirement of having a vision. The writer says believers have already received Christ and have been identified with him in baptism (2:6-7, 11-12). They need no more than this because identification with him brings them into the one who has "all the fullness of divinity" (2:9). Thus, they have already received the forgiveness that prohibits anyone from condemning them (2:13-16). In addition, the rules that the other teachers advocate are ineffective in promoting ethical living, so they should be rejected (2:22-23).

After having rejected the other teaching's demands about behavior, the writer makes it clear that the faith does include ethical demands. In a surprising turn of phrase, after telling the readers not to seek visions for most of the letter, at 3:1 he tells them to "seek the things that are above." What follows are instructions about how to live in the world as a believer. Seeking the things above becomes living as a person whose life is "hidden with Christ in God" (3:3). The instructions that follow indicate clearly that all of life is to be governed by the gifts one receives at baptism. Such instructions obviate the need for the ascetic and ritual demands of the visionaries.

Watching the Writer of Colossians Work

Colossians uses a number of powerful arguments to persuade the readers not to accept the teaching of the visionaries. An important argument employs a liturgy to express a Christology that renders irrelevant any call for attention to or from angelic beings. This liturgy (which is often called a hymn) appears in 1:15-20. It identifies Christ as God's agent in the creation of all things, including angelic powers. It identifies Christ as the one in whom God's fullness is found. Thus, connection with Christ brings all the spiritual blessings one could possibly attain. Further, Christ is the one through whom God reconciles all things. The writer introduces this liturgy by reminding the readers that they already enjoy forgiveness and spiritual blessings from God (1:12-14). Inserting the liturgy about Christ reminds them that there can be no more powerful agent through whom they can receive God's blessings and forgiveness.

After the liturgy, the only condition for retaining the blessings that come from the most powerful being in the cosmos is that they remain faithful to the teaching they first received. Thus, they must reject the other, more recent, teaching. The author seems to assume that the readers know and use this liturgy. Its familiarity is part of what makes it persuasive. Its presence allows him to imply that they already believe what he advocates. The conflict Colossians sets up between this view of the work of Christ and the other teaching implies that the latter contradicts the central teachings that they had already accepted. This tacit contradiction becomes more explicit in the immediately following verses where it says that their blamelessness at judgment depends upon them remaining faithful to the original teaching they had received (2:21-23).

Thus, the liturgy serves two purposes. First, it brings to mind a belief that they affirm in their use of the liturgy. It reminds them of what they confess about Christ and what he accomplishes for them. They will likely not have recognized the contradiction between this confession and the teaching of the visionaries, but its citation between two affirmations of their forgiveness and salvation would begin to help them see the tension. Second, the explicit instruction to remain faithful to the original teaching, teaching encapsulated in part in the liturgy, more directly argues against accepting the new doctrine.

While the liturgy of 1:15-20 has often been used as a basis for the church's Christology, its purpose here is not to offer teaching about the nature and work of Christ. Christology is not an issue in the church Colossians addresses. The writer assumes that all the readers agree with what is said about Christ in the liturgy. Only if this is the case does it provide good grounds for rejecting the visionaries' teaching.

The call to remain faithful to the original message reappears as the central polemical section of the letter opens. In 2:6-7, the writer contrasts remaining faithful to what they were originally taught with the new teaching. The options are to continue in Christ or be tricked into accepting deceitful human tradition (2:6-8). Further on in the section the options are remaining identified with Christ and his death or taking on commandments that come from human authorities, even if they seem to have backing from higher powers (2:20-23). These ways of setting out the contrasts make one option far more appealing and really the only viable option.

Ethos also plays a major role in the argument of Colossians. The central affirmation of 1:24-2:5 is that Paul is the reliable teacher to whom they should listen. He has been commissioned by God to bring the gospel to them and he is the one who is willing to suffer for their good. In the most dramatic language in the Pauline corpus about Paul's suffering for his churches, Colossians says that Paul "fill[s] up what is lacking in the afflictions of Christ" for the church (1:24). This language seems to mean that Paul is willing to give a living and observable example of the way Christ acted for others. Thus, while Christ's sufferings dealt with sin, Paul's sufferings provide an immediate example of the way Christ lived his life for the good of others. This passage is most powerful if it is written after Paul's death, when this way of living had led him to give his life as Christ gave his life. But whether Paul is alive or a martyr, this description of him sets him apart as the person who cares the most for the readers. His suffering for them suggests that he is the most reliable teacher, so they should listen to him. This argument from ethos carries a significant amount of the burden of the letter's argument.

A third kind of major argument in Colossians is its explication of the meaning of baptism. From 2:11 to at least 3:14, images of baptism undergird the instructions about rejecting the visionaries' teaching. Baptism is their covenant initiation, as circumcision had been for Judaism (2:11-14). In the same verses baptism brings a participation in the death of Christ and a being raised to new life with sins forgiven. Since this is the case, the rules of the other teachers are not needed. The image of dying with Christ reappears in 2:20, and being raised with him recurs in 3:1. The affirmations of death to the old life and being raised to new life give way to exhortation in 3:5. Here believers are to "put to death" immoral behavior because in baptism they have died to that life.

The language of changing clothes was also associated with baptism in the early church. By sometime in the second century, initiates took off their clothes to be baptized and were then dressed in new clothes to signal their new identity. In the Roman era, a person's dress was an indication of their social identity. There were even some kinds of clothing that only upper-class people were allowed to wear. So the image of putting on different clothes was powerful. Colossians asserts that believers have already been clothed with a new self (3:9-10). Since they already possess this new identity, they have no need of the new teaching. All of these references and allusions to baptism point to an event in the past that gives the readers everything the visionaries claim is gained through their teaching. So this interpretation of the readers' own experience of baptism shows that they should reject the condemnation and so the demands of the other teachers.

All of Colossians's emphasis on what believers already possess makes its eschatology distinctive when compared to the undisputed letters. All of the Pauline letters have some element of realized eschatology. Paul constantly recognizes the Spirit as a gift of the end time that believers now possess. But the undisputed letters also emphasize the coming fulfillment at the parousia. In Colossians there is a shift in the balance; there is more emphasis on present possession and less on future elements. While in Romans believers have died with Christ so that they might live in newness of life while looking to the resurrection that is to come (6:3-5), in Colossians believers have already been raised with Christ (3:1; see also 2:12). Colossians also asserts that believers have fullness in Christ in the present (2:9-10). Colossians still looks forward to the Second Coming (1:5; 3:4; 3:24–4:1), but realized elements of eschatology gain prominence.

This shift in emphasis is due at least in part to the nature of the problem Colossians addresses. The other teachers contend that those without visionary experiences remain in sin and lack the spiritual blessings that those who have visions possess. Colossians responds by asserting that all believers, through their relationship with Christ and God that is gained at baptism, already possess all the spiritual blessings that are available in the present. Its realized eschatology, then, is a part of the claim that believers enjoy these blessings through baptism without the visionaries' demands. Given this purpose, it is not clear whether the basic eschatology of the author of Colossians is different from that of the undisputed letters or whether the difference is the result of addressing a problem that demanded a different kind of response.

Colossians seldom bases an argument on scripture. When it does, that scripture is mediated through the church's tradition. So the traditional material Colossians cites (the liturgy and other materials scattered throughout the letter, e.g., its use of a baptismal liturgy in 3:11) serves as an important authority. While the undisputed letters cite traditional material, they also cite scripture. This reliance on tradition nearly to the exclusion of any citation of scripture is another factor that makes Colossians distinctive.

Theology in Colossians

Colossians interprets the church's traditions about Christ and baptism to call its readers to reject the teaching of those who call for a regime of observances designed to enable visionary experiences that are evidence of or that impart forgiveness and relationship with God. Its author contends that those observances are unnecessary because baptized believers already possess all the spiritual gifts the other teachers promise. Colossians emphasizes the present possession of eschatological gifts to bolster its argument. The gifts of God are not just promises about the future; the baptized possess them now in the fullest measure they can be received in the present.

The argument of Colossians relies on its Christology, a Christology that it does not argue for but expects its readers to affirm already. The liturgical section (1:15-20) provides the theological basis for the claims the letter makes about receiving the forgiveness and access to all blessings without the other teachers' regulations. That liturgy identifies Christ as God's agent in the creation of all things and as the one through whom believers receive peace with God. Thus, it expects its recipients to have a complex Christology that includes the preexistence of Christ and his centrality for securing and maintaining a place with God now and after God's final eschatological victory.

Baptism emerges as a central rite of the church. It is the moment at which one receives forgiveness and is inducted into the people of God. It is the covenant sign that can assure believers that they have the right relationship with God, the relationship that grants salvation and all spiritual blessings. Baptism grants a new identity with Christ that gives full possession of those blessings. As believers are incorporated into Christ and so given a new identity at baptism, their old selves are put to death and they are given new life. This gift of new life with its many blessings also demands that believers live in ways that are consistent with their new identity. The gift of new life grounds the letter's ethical exhortations.

The theological themes of the letter (including its interpretation of baptism) are explications of the claims made about Christ in the liturgy. This is an effective strategy because the writer assumes that the readers already accept the liturgy as true. With that common ground, this letter points to the sufficiency of Christ as the sole necessary and possible means of attaining forgiveness, a relationship with God, and all spiritual blessings.

Suggested Reading

Markus Barth and Helmut Blanke. *Colossians: A New Translation with Introduction and Commentary*. Anchor Bible. New York: Doubleday, 1994.

David M. Hay. *Colossians*. Abingdon New Testament Commentaries. Nashville: Abingdon, 2000.

Andrew T. Lincoln and A. J. M. Wedderburn. *The Theology of the Later Pauline Letters*. New Testament Theology. Cambridge: Cambridge University Press, 1993.

Margaret Y. MacDonald. *Colossians and Ephesians*. Sacra Pagina. Collegeville, MN.: Liturgical Press, 2000.

Jerry L. Sumney. *Colossians: A Commentary*. New Testament Library. Louisville: Westminster John Knox, 2008.

Brian J. Walsh and Sylvia C. Keesmaat. *Colossians Remixed: Subverting the Empire*. Downers Grove: IVP Academic, 2004.

Harry O. Maier. *Picturing Paul in Empire: Imperial Image, Text and Persuasion in Colossians, Ephesians and the Pastoral Epistles*. New York: Bloomsbury T. & T. Clark, 2013.

Chapter 12

SECOND THESSALONIANS

———— ·❧· ————

The Second Coming Is Still to Come

About half of critical scholars think that 2 Thessalonians is pseudony-mous. The language and style are compatible with Paul's genuine letters, but the parallels between it and 1 Thessalonians are so close that it seems the writer of 2 Thessalonians has copied the outline of 1 Thessalonians. In fact, there seems to be a parallel in 2 Thessalonians for every paragraph in 1 Thessalonians. In addition, the greeting of 2 Thessalonians is word-for-word the same (except for one word) as in 1 Thessalonians. No genuine Pauline greetings are so much alike.

Beyond these matters of style, the text of 2 Thessalonians actually raises the question of authenticity. In 2:2, the writer cautions readers not to listen to letters that purport to come from Paul. Then the end of the letter claims to have Paul's signature (3:17). Given that all the circulating Pauline letters were copied by people other than the originating author, such a claim could only be verified if someone possessed the autograph—which we do not have, and neither did most early readers. This constellation of concerns raises the question of whether the letter was written by Paul or after his death. We will treat it as a letter written a few years after his death.

Practical Problems and Responses

Second Thessalonians addresses a community experiencing persecution. The most likely type of affliction is social and economic ostracizing. The writer calls the readers to remain faithful by reminding them of the eschatological scenario that Paul had always taught. He recalls the coming judgment in which believers will be glorified (1:12) and those who persecute them will be punished (1:5-10). While the pattern is Pauline, the emphasis on the coming punishment of those who afflict the readers is not what we expect in Paul. This letter dwells more on the punishment of persecutors than do the undisputed letters.

The second, and seemingly central, issue that 2 Thessalonians addresses concerns the timing and nature of the Second Coming. Some are teaching that "the day of the Lord is already here" (2:2). Earlier interpreters sought ways by which they could interpret these words to mean that the teaching said that the Day of the Lord is *near*. This would make the problem much like that of 1 Thessalonians, where the people wonder why Christ's Second Coming has not happened before anyone in their church died. But the language clearly indicates that the teaching asserts that the Day of the Lord has already come. Thus, its advocates have redefined the Day of the Lord so that it is a kind of spiritual experience, an experience that only some of them have attained, while others continue to look for its coming. The problem 2 Thessalonians addresses, then, is quite different from that of 1 Thessalonians.

The teaching 2 Thessalonians opposes is an overrealized eschatology. This eschatology claims that some people possess more of the gifts and presence of God than the author thinks anyone can have at the present. Paul consistently has a partially realized eschatology. He asserts that some gifts of the end time are already available to believers, even as they must wait to receive their fullness until the catastrophic intervention by God that defeats evil and brings God's people fully into God's presence. Because those whom 2 Thessalonians opposes claim to have more gifts than the author thinks are available, they have, in his view, an *over*realized eschatology.

The writer draws on elements of the readers' eschatology that are not in question to remind them that he (as Paul) had told them that certain things had to happen before the end came. Since these historical events have not happened, the claim that the Day of the Lord is already here must be false. It is important for the author to speak as Paul here because the other teaching seems to have relied on the Spirit and on a letter claiming to be from Paul (2:2). The claim that this letter's teaching is the genuine Paul comes not only from the letter's greeting, but also in 2:15 where the writer says that the view the letter supports is consistent with what Paul taught in person and in other letters.

This issue is important because of what it says about the nature of God's eschatological act. If the other teachers are correct, then the end time act of God involves only the spiritual experience of individuals in the present. The author of 2 Thessalonians thinks that is too small to capture what God intends. For him, the parousia is a cosmic event in which God reclaims all that exists. It is the moment of the defeat of evil and of the overwhelming victory of God over all that diminishes life. This view of the end is a central element of the church's eschatology from its earliest years, and the writer of 2 Thessalonians is unwilling to reduce it to personal experience. So a great deal is at stake in this exchange.

The main practical consequence of the belief that the Day of the Lord is already present is that some in the church have quit their regular jobs and have devoted themselves to work in the church. They have appointed themselves ministers because they have the extraordinary experience of participating in the Day of the Lord. Thinking they possess superior qualifications, they demand financial support from the church (3:6-13). The nature of this problem is obscured by the translation tradition of the section that deals with the problem. The NRSV follows this tradition by rendering the word *ataktoi* as "idleness" throughout the section. But the term *ataktoi* actually means "disorderly," not idle. The people disturbing the church are not doing nothing, not living in idleness, but are "busybodies" (3:11). Their disorderly behavior is disrupting the church's life. The writer says that the pattern of Paul working while he conducts his ministry is the example these people should follow rather than demanding support from the church (3:8-10). These people have not quit their jobs to wait for Jesus to appear in the clouds; they have quit their jobs to devote themselves to ministry because they have a superior experience of the presence of God. This superiority, they think, permits them to impose their service on the church and to demand support. The writer of 2 Thessalonians rejects both the claim of superior experience (because the Day has not come) and the pattern of ministry they have adopted. He tells the church to stop giving these people money. When he says, "If they won't work, don't give them anything to eat" (v. 10, paraphrased), he does not mean the church should stop helping the poor; rather he is telling the readers they should not comply with the demands of these self-appointed leaders.

The central issue of 2 Thessalonians, then, is overrealized eschatology and the theological and ministerial consequences some draw from that belief. The writer of the letter rejects both the eschatology and the corollaries drawn from it.

Watching the Writer of 2 Thessalonians Work

One of the most important arguments the author of 2 Thessalonians employs is that of identifying his eschatology with the apostolic teaching. He assumes that everyone thinks that it is important to be consistent with Paul's teaching. This is implied when he notes that those who advocate the alternative eschatology claim that it comes from a letter of Paul (2:2). The writer calls the readers to retain the true apostolic teaching (2:15). The central support for the claim that this letter contains that correct teaching is that it is genuinely from the Apostle Paul. At the same time, he says the other teachers' claim to be apostolic is a deception (2:2-3). This letter is genuine because it bears Paul's signature, and does so in the way that Paul signs "every letter" (3:17).

The second way the author draws on apostolic authority is by citing the pattern of Paul's ministry. A crucial argument against the other teachers' demand for financial support is that Paul always worked at a trade while serving as a missionary. This apostolic pattern becomes the approved way of conducting ministry for this church.

Another major type of argument this author makes is that his position is in accord with other elements of eschatology that the readers still maintain. He reminds them that the coming judgment will punish those who now persecute them (1:5-10). This provides a powerful incentive to maintain the belief that the Second Coming is still in the future; otherwise the wicked escape any repercussions of the evil committed against God's faithful. Thus, the tradition's belief that the Second Coming includes a coming judgment supports the writer's eschatological scheme, while making the other view less attractive.

More directly, this author claims that his view coheres with what the Thessalonians have been taught about what must take place before the parousia. The references to the "person of lawlessness" and the one who holds him back (2:7-8) are oblique to current readers, but these must have been familiar to the original readers. These symbolic names probably apply to specific historical figures of the first century. If so, they know that the events the tradition names have not transpired.

The author bolsters this argument about what must happen before the Second Coming by associating it with a tradition in Daniel that is well known in the first century. In Daniel 11–12 there is a symbolic description of the desecration of the Jerusalem temple by Antiochus IV (167 BCE). His act of desecration and its description in Daniel enter the apocalyptic tradition as a pattern for describing the acts of the wicked against the people of God, particularly threats to the integrity of the temple. At least one emperor had threatened to put an image in the Jerusalem temple, but the deed was never accomplished. This allusion to defiling the temple suggests that 2 Thessalonians was written either before the temple was destroyed or that the author sets it within the lifetime of Paul. Either way it counters the view that says that the Day of the Lord has already come. If the temple is still standing, it is obvious that the time has not come. If the temple has fallen, this letter still claims to be written in Paul's time when the temple was standing. In this case, the writer expects the readers to see that the same teaching they now face was rejected earlier by Paul and for good reason. Even if the temple has fallen, the "person of lawlessness" is still being held back.

The most important arguments this author uses to persuade the recipients of this letter to reject the overrealized eschatology relate to retaining the church's traditions. The central claim is that the letter contains the apostolic teaching. This letter assumes that Pauline authorship guarantees correctness. But also important is the reinforcement of this correctness by connecting it to elements of the church's eschatology that remain important to a persecuted church. Only the traditional eschatological scheme helps them interpret the seeming success of their persecutors and assures them of their salvation despite their painful experiences. These ways of arguing suggest that the battle over the authority of Paul is past so that he is now revered as an authority. This suggests that 2 Thessalonians was written after Paul's death.

What We Learn about the Theology of 2 Thessalonians

Few elements of this author's theology come into clear view except his eschatology. He clearly thinks that a future aspect of theology is critical to the faith. A future catastrophic event that brings judgment on persecutors and vindicates the faithful supports faith in the one God who is just and powerful. He also sees the coming judgment as the act of a loving God who refuses to allow God's own to be abused without there being some repercussions. He seems to see this future validation of the faith as something that will encourage faithfulness in the present. Alternatively, to think that the Second

Coming has already happened could lead to discouragement because their suffering then has no response from God.

Apostolic authority is crucial for this writer's theological reasoning. This letter relies on that authority more than any of the undisputed letters. In the undisputed letters, Paul must often convince the readers of his authority. In 2 Thessalonians, that authority is assumed. The author provides other supporting arguments, but the pivotal sanction for its instructions is that they come from the apostle. Not only are the apostle's teachings authoritative, so is his example. His pattern of ministry is the authorized pattern of ministry for the church. This argument, of course, appears often in the undisputed letters. In 2 Thessalonians, however, there is more of an assumption that Paul's example is authoritative. Apostolicity, then, has become a dominant criterion for evaluating teaching and behavior in the church of 2 Thessalonians.

Suggested Reading

Victor Paul Furnish. *1 & 2 Thessalonians*. Abingdon New Testament Commentary. Nashville: Abingdon, 2007.

Beverley Roberts Gaventa. *First and Second Thessalonians*. Interpretation. Louisville: Westminster, 2012.

Abraham J. Malherbe. *The Letters to the Thessalonians: A New Translation with Introduction and Commentary*. Anchor Bible. New York: Doubleday, 2000.

Earl J. Richard. *First and Second Thessalonians*. Sacra Pagina. Wilmington: Michael Glazier, 2007.

Chapter 13

EPHESIANS

Maintaining the Unity of the Church

A large majority of scholars identify Ephesians as pseudonymous and probably written near the end of the first century. It addresses a later time in the life of the church when the dispute over whether Gentiles should keep those parts of the law that designate people as Jews is no longer raging for this author; rather, as we will see, his concern is to keep Gentile believers and Jewish believers in Christ within the same church.

Ephesians has a new vision of the meaning of the church as the body of Christ. While the undisputed Pauline letters routinely refer to a single congregation (or perhaps the congregations in a city) as a "body," in Ephesians the church worldwide is the body of Christ (5:25). Ephesians also speaks of apostles in ways it is hard to imagine Paul referring to them. In Galatians, Paul notes that some consider the Jerusalem apostles the pillars of the church, but he comments that that means nothing to him. In Ephesians, however, apostles are the foundation of the church (2:20). Indeed, they are the "holy apostles" to whom the gospel has been revealed (3:5).

Most interpreters also believe there is some literary relationship between Colossians and Ephesians. Most think Ephesians borrowed from Colossians, particularly in the way that Ephesians adds onto some already rather lengthy phrases in Colossians. Ephesians copies these and then adds a few words of its own. It is also notable that Ephesians has even more emphasis on the realized aspect of eschatology than does Colossians.

Our earliest copies of Ephesians lack an address. Where the text now reads "To the saints who are in Ephesus and faithful in Christ Jesus" there was once no place name given, so the greeting read simply, "To the saints who are faithful in Christ." This has led some to speculate that Ephesians was originally a circular letter. That may be more than the evidence will bear, but the occasion of the letter does seem less specific than what we find in other Pauline letters. Even though its occasion seems less specific, it is concerned about some specific issues.

Practical Problems and Responses

Ephesians has a dominant central issue to which it devotes most of its attention: the unity of the church. The particular question involves the relationship between Jewish and Gentile members. The letter seems to come from a time when the church is beginning to think of itself as an entity that is detached from Judaism. The author is concerned that Gentiles not see the church as separated from its roots in Judaism and perhaps that Jews do not see the Gentile believers as secondary to the identity of the church. The primary audience of the letter, though, is Gentiles.

Ephesians addresses the issue of the unity of Jewish and Gentile believers most explicitly in 2:11-22. In verse 11, the author uses a dismissive term to refer to non-Jews; he notes that some call them "the uncircumcision." Such language only comes from those who see Gentiles as outside the covenant with God. The author writes as a Jew, reminding the readers that "you" (Gentiles) were aliens and strangers to the covenant, people who were without God (2:12). He usually maintains the distinction between Jews and Gentiles outside of Christ, but on occasion he groups all people together as those in need of the gospel. In 2:3, after noting in the previous verses that "you" were dead through sin, he says that "*we* were by nature children of wrath, just like the rest" (emphasis added). This universal need for the gospel provides a basis for unity. Later in the letter he notes that God, as father, gives all ethnic groups their name (3:14-15). But such expressions of a natural oneness are rare in Ephesians (or in any of the New Testament). Most often Jews are seen as the covenant people while Gentiles outside the church are separated from God and living in sin (e.g., 2:1-2, 11-13, 19; 3:17-19; 4:17-19).

Ephesians proclaims that the division and accompanying hostility between Jews and Gentiles is overcome in Christ because both receive salvation in Christ. In a few places, Jews and Gentiles seem to come to this salvation as equals. For example, in 1:5, all are adopted by God and made heirs. But the usual perspective is that Gentiles are brought into the blessings of Israel. For example, in 2:19, Gentiles are made members of the household of God after being strangers to the commonwealth of Israel. One of the clearest statements of this perspective appears in 3:5-6, where the mystery hidden for ages and finally revealed in the last days is that Gentiles are brought into God's family as fellow heirs with Jews. But this happens only in Christ.

This perspective maintains the priority of Israel in salvation. Through Christ Gentiles are brought to enjoy the blessings that believing Israelites already had as children of God. The work of Christ does even more to establish unity between Jews and Gentiles. By bringing both into the family of God and giving salvation to both, the work of Christ also puts an end to the hostility between the two. Ephesians says that the work of Christ ended the hostility by abolishing the law. This is a more radical statement about the law than anything in the undisputed Paulines. While Paul refuses to allow Gentiles to adopt the distinctive identity markers of Jews, he does not say that the law has been abolished. It still has important functions for Paul. But Ephesians contends that it is abolished so that Jews and Gentiles can live together as one. Rejection of those commands allows a common life together for Jews and Gentiles. Still, as the covenant people, Jews have a priority in salvation.

Ephesians responds further to the continuing distinction that threatens church unity by emphasizing how much Jewish and Gentile church members have in common. Most important, all have been saved only through Christ (1:3-12 [note the use of "we" and "us"]; 2:6-10, 13). Additionally, the well-known list in 4:4-5 names things all believers share (one body, Spirit, hope, Lord, faith, baptism, God); these shared things create and manifest a deep unity. All also exist together as the one body of Christ (4:14-16). Additionally, the whole church depends on the apostles. Indeed, Christ bestowing the gift of apostleship on some people brings unity to the church (4:13; see also 2:19-20).

Ephesians must also deal with two related issues: the absence of Paul and the delay in the parousia. Ephesians identifies Paul as *the* apostle to the Gentiles, as the one chosen by God for this task (3:1-4, 7-13). As one who suffers and is imprisoned for them, Paul exhorts them to live in unity (3:13; 4:1-3). Since the original readers see the letter only after Paul has been martyred, this exhortation bears even more weight. Attention to his suffering while alive helps the readers interpret his death. Furthermore, if his testimony was weighty because he was willing to suffer for the gospel and for his Gentile converts, it is even more powerful when he is a martyr.

The delay in the parousia has not only deprived the church of Paul but also has made many wonder how they should live in the world. The imminent expectation of the parousia might suggest some ways of living that seem impractical in the long term. As we saw with Colossians, the Second Coming's delay has led to an emphasis on the realized aspects of eschatology and to more spatial imagery in relation to eschatological gifts.

The emphasis on realized eschatology begins with the opening blessing of Ephesians. At 1:3, the author asserts that in Christ believers already possess "every spiritual blessing in the heavenly places," and a few lines later they have already obtained an inheritance (1:11). Indeed believers are already seated with Christ in the heavenly places (2:6). Unity is another element of the eschatological life that they now enjoy. The hidden mystery that is revealed and manifested is the unity of Jews and Gentiles in the church (3:5-6). So this emphasis on realized eschatology also supports the central theme of the letter.

While emphasizing the present possession of eschatological gifts, the writer also looks forward to experiencing the fullness of the blessings that they now possess only partially. The eschatological gift of the Spirit (a realized aspect of eschatology) is the promise of future blessings at the Second Coming (1:13-14; 4:30). The threat of coming judgment also plays a part in Ephesians's exhortations (5:5). So even though the emphasis is clearly on the realized elements of eschatological existence, Ephesians has not lost sight of a future aspect of eschatology.

As the mention of judgment suggests, ethics and eschatology are related in Ephesians. The delay in the parousia requires the church to think about its place in the world. How does it relate to the structures of society and culture? How, if at all, should it stand apart from the rest of the world? Obviously they must reject the worship of other gods, but what about the believer's personal morality, and what about his or her household?

With an eye toward the already possessed eschatological blessings, the coming judgment, and the character of God, Ephesians calls its readers to take their ethical lives seriously. It describes believers as so distinct from their surroundings that they have been given a new self (4:17-24). Yet many of the virtues Ephesians advocates were also recommended by the moral philosophers of the day. A number of interpreters see Ephesians taking a step back from some more radical egalitarian notions found in the undisputed letters. This is particularly the case with the household code. It seems to insist on imposing the cultural expectations of the roles of wives and slaves on members of the church. Some interpreters see elements that soften the subordination of women, children, and slaves, particularly the call for mutual submission in 5:21. But the writer of Ephesians seems more comfortable with the traditional household structure than do Paul and the author of Colossians. On the other hand, the author tells the readers to separate themselves from the world and to be on guard against its evils (e.g., 6:10-17). Looking to the long-term existence of the church in the world, Ephesians senses less tension between the values of the kingdom of God and those of the culture; still, the author draws clear lines between the church and the rest of the world. The continuing presence of the church in the world may demand a less oppositional stance to make life less difficult, but the church is still distinct from the world.

Watching the Writer of Ephesians Work

The most obvious persuasive technique Ephesians employs is claiming to be written by Paul. Such a claim grants its instructions apostolic authority, but even more than that, Paul is not just one of the apostles to whom the eschatological message of the gospel has been revealed (3:5) and on whom the church is built (2:19-20), he is specifically the apostle to the Gentiles (3:1-4). As the apostle divinely dispatched to the letter's readers, he has yet more authority. In addition, he is willing to suffer for them and for what they hold dear (3:13; 4:1). As we noted above, since Paul's suffering has culminated in his martyrdom, his instructions carry more weight because he was willing to die for the gospel and the good of those to whom he was commissioned. So the first and most evident element of persuasion is an argument from ethos. They should listen to Paul because he has their good at heart and because he has authority from God.

Less specific, but still an argument from ethos, is the identification of the author as a Jew. Within the early church, it was assumed that Jews had more knowledge of God and God's will than Gentiles. Not only had Jews grown up with belief in the one God, they were also the ones who knew the Bible. By the time of Ephesians there are Gentiles who have grown up in the church, but the status of Jews within the church seems to have been maintained even among Gentile congregations. Seemingly without expecting any disagreement, Jews are identified as those who were "near" and who already have the covenants of promise (2:11-14). It remains surprising that the gospel makes Gentiles fellow heirs with Israel (3:5-6). So having the author speak as a Jewish believer in Christ addressing Gentile believers gives the author authority.

This author also cites church tradition as an authority to support his call for unity and for his ethical instructions. At times the citation of traditions provides a kind of general credibility. The quotation of the tradition about the exaltation of Christ in 1:20-22 (23) does not directly support a point of the argument, but it assures the readers that the author holds the same core beliefs they hold. In this way it prepares the readers to accept what the writer recommends.

In other places the traditional material provides more direct support for points in the letter's argument. The author cites a confessional formula in 2:14-18 to make his central point: Gentiles and Jews live in unity because all have access to God through Christ. Ephesians interprets the citation in verse 19 by saying that Gentiles are now "citizens with the saints" and members of God's household with Jews. A confession the readers already accept, then, serves an important role in moving the readers to recognize the unity of Jews and Gentiles in the church.

Unlike Colossians, Ephesians also cites scripture. Sometimes these citations are identified as scripture with an introductory formula (e.g., 4:7-8), but at other times they are not (e.g., 5:31). The quotation of Psalm 68:18 in 4:8 provides support for the recognition of diverse gifts within the church. This only indirectly supports the call for unity, but the citation of Isaiah 57:19 in 2:17 explicitly interprets the work of Christ as the means through which God has brought Jews and Gentiles together and has given both access to God. Similarly, instructions about the relationship between husband and wife in 5:29-31 cites Genesis 2:24. It is impossible to know whether the readers would have recognized all the citations of scripture or how many of them were mediated by the tradition rather than being known as biblical texts. But even if the auditors do not recognize every citation, scripture serves as a significant authority for this author. It provides proofs for various positions he advocates. While he does not use it extensively, it supports his positions in several places, some of which are peripheral to the central issues and others that lie at the heart of his argument.

Most often Ephesians mounts theological arguments drawn from christological and eschatological affirmations. God's exaltation of Christ to a place that is above all (1:20-23) puts both Jews and Gentiles under Christ's authority. More specifically, God raised "us" (Jewish and Gentile believers) with Christ and placed "us" in the heavenly places with him (2:4-7). This first person plural ("us") appears in a passage where the author has designated Gentiles as "you." But when he speaks of the salvation believers receive in Christ, the pronoun becomes "us," signaling that both Jews and Gentiles are included. That meaning becomes explicit in the next paragraph when those who were far away (Gentiles) are brought into the blessings of Israel through the death of Christ (2:11-13). Indeed, Gentiles are now citizens of God's realm and members of God's household with Jews (2:19).

A further implication the author draws from Christ's death is that it eliminates the hostility between Jews and Gentiles by abolishing the law, thus creating a single humanity in Christ (2:14-18). This view simplifies the Pauline view of the law and of ethnic identity in the church. In the undisputed letters, Gentiles remain Gentiles and Jews remain Jews, which means that the latter continue to observe the law. But here the death of Christ effects the reconciliation of the two by eliminating the thing that separated them, the law. With this outlook, Ephesians affirms Jewish identity by assuming that Jews are the chosen people of God, those who are God's household, but jettisons the means by which they express that identity.

The importance of the eschatological nature of Christ's work is evident in the definition Ephesians gives to the end-time mystery that it accomplishes: Gentiles are brought into the people of God, into the family of God, a family that had previously been composed of Jews (3:1-6). The letter's emphasis on present possession of eschatological gifts raises the stakes of the discussion. Participation in the eschatological mystery brings blessings the readers want (salvation, relationship with God, the Spirit, a place in the "heavenly places"). At the same time it includes reconciliation between Jewish and Gentile believers. Tying these two things together is a powerful move because the readers are not willing to relinquish their relationship with God and the promises and experiences it provides. Now those indispensable things are linked to participation of Gentiles and Jews in God's family and nation and are inextricably connected to reconciliation of the two. Thus, Gentiles' present participation in the gifts of God depends on their continued relationship with God's historic people. This is a powerful argument for the unity for which Ephesians calls.

As it has been with other letters, Ephesians uses a number of persuasive strategies to move its readers to adopt the positions it advocates. Its use of tradition is more extensive than in the undisputed letters, but is similar to Colossians. But Ephesians uses scripture as an authority in ways that are more similar to the authentic letters. Its emphasis on realized eschatology helps the author secure acceptance of his call to unity because the readers do not want to lose what they have in Christ. So the unity the author wants the church to recognize and accept is made a necessary part of what the readers see as crucial advantages of being members of the church.

What We Learn about the Theology of Ephesians

The theological arguments that bear the most weight in Ephesians are its Christology and its identification of God as creator/father and as the one who exalted Christ. This author identifies Christ as the one who has been appointed ruler of all things and so is in position to grant Gentiles a place with God that gives them equal possession of the blessings of salvation (1:17-23). Even more, he is the domain in which all things, including salvation and eschatological gifts, dwell (1:5-14). It is through identification with him and inclusion within his body that Jews and Gentiles are made one (4:11-16). The salvation found in Christ includes the reconciliation of the two groups and the abolition of the law (2:12-18). Indeed, a central element in the "mystery of Christ" is that Gentiles are fellow heirs and members of the same body as Jews.

While emphasizing what is gained in Christ, Ephesians does not lose sight of God as the originator of salvation. Christ is in the position he has because God has placed him there. Christ remains God's agent in salvation. God blesses and chooses all for salvation through Christ (1:3-6). It is God's wisdom that is seen in the unity of Jews and Gentiles (1:8-10) and God who raised believers in Christ to salvation (2:4-10). It is also God who commissions Paul to be the apostle to Gentiles (3:7-10).

In addition to being the foundational power behind salvation, God is also the author of the unity Ephesians advocates because God is the creator of all. In one of the few places at which Ephesians finds a oneness of Jews and Gentiles outside of Christ, the author identifies God as the father of all families (NRSV), that is, of all ethnic identifications, all those of earth and of the heavens (3:14). All are named, and so claimed, by God. This creates a unity of all people as children of God.

Ephesians, then, relies heavily on the identity it asserts for God and on the identity and work of Christ. The description of the salvation that all believers share because of these characteristics and acts of God, and most often those acts accomplished through Christ, creates and demands recognition of the unity of all believers.

Suggested Reading

Ernest Best. *Ephesians: A Shorter Commentary*. Edinburgh: Bloomsbury T. & T. Clark, 2003.

Bonnie Bowman Thurston. *Reading Colossians, Ephesians, and 2 Thessalonians: A Literary and Theological Commentary*. New York: Crossroad, 1995.

Lewis R. Donelson. *Colossians, Ephesians, First and Second Timothy, and Titus*. Westminster Bible Companion. Louisville: Westminster John Knox, 1996.

Andrew T. Lincoln. *Ephesians*. Word Biblical Commentary. Dallas: Word, 1990.

Andrew T. Lincoln and A. J. M. Wedderburn. *The Theology of the Later Pauline Letters*. New Testament Theology. Cambridge: Cambridge University Press, 1993.

Margaret Y. MacDonald. *Colossians and Ephesians*. Sacra Pagina. Collegeville, MN.: Liturgical Press, 2000.

Harry O. Maier. *Picturing Paul in Empire: Imperial Image, Text and Persuasion in Colossians, Ephesians and the Pastoral Epistles*. New York: Bloomsbury T. & T. Clark, 2013.

Chapter 14
THE PASTORAL EPISTLES

Equipping the Church for Long-Term Faithfulness

The Pastoral Epistles are three short letters purportedly written by Paul to junior associates. They authorize these leaders to address issues in the churches with which they are working. Critical scholars are nearly unanimous in saying that Paul did not write the Pastoral Epistles. Not only are the style and theology different from the undisputed letters, but they also seem to come from a later time. Furthermore, they seem to assume that Paul was released from prison in Rome and then returned to Asia Minor and Greece rather than going on to Spain, which he announced as his plan when he wrote Romans (15:18-24). Most interpreters think Paul was executed in Rome rather than gaining his freedom only to be arrested again and then executed.

A number of interpreters argue that the three Pastoral Epistles all address the same situation and are written by the same author at about the same time. Our treatment will not make those assumptions. We will treat each letter individually, seeing what problems it addresses, what responses it proffers, and how it makes the case for its positions.

1 Timothy

Practical Problems and Responses

First Timothy addresses two central issues: a false teaching and the influence of the "widows." The opposed teaching interprets the law in a way that

155

1 Timothy rejects. The teachers' abstinence from some foods may be related to their interpretation of the law. But they also advocate some rejection of marriage (4:3-5). It is less clear how this might be related to their reading of scripture. Still, they attach at least some of their teaching to observance of the law. Unlike Ephesians, the author does not say that the law has been abolished; rather, 1 Timothy limits the function of the law and calls for proper interpretation. The author says the law is good and serves to control immoral people whose conduct violates the gospel (1:8-11).

The opposing teachers seem to refer to their teaching as "knowledge" (6:20). Many earlier interpreters used this label to identify them as Gnostics. This was especially popular following the discovery of the Nag Hammadi library. But many groups referred to their teaching as knowledge, so this is an insufficient basis on which to make such an identification. Some of the teachings that 1 Timothy opposes may have become a part of the later, more systematic presentations of Gnosticism, but the text does not support identifying these teachers with any such elaborate system. Furthermore, the charge that they require abstinence from marriage may well not represent a balanced characterization of their teaching. This element of their theology may be related to the issues about "widows," as we will see below.

The author denigrates this teaching by calling it a myth and saying it is just prattling about genealogies rather than being concerned with important things (1:4). Indeed the teaching is "godless myths and wives' tales" (4:7). The author further accuses the other teachers of craving controversies and disputes over unimportant matters, asserting that such teaching leads to all sorts of vices (6:4-5). This disparaging of the other teaching intends to make it unattractive.

The author is so concerned about proper teaching because he believes that false teaching leads to immoral living (1:5-7, 18-20; 6:10). On the other hand, those who hold correct teaching also lead good lives (1:6, 19). In 6:5-6, "piety" (what the NRSV translates as "godliness) or proper living even seems to represent the content of the faith. This letter, then, stresses the relationship between doctrine and ethics.

The second issue this letter addresses involves "widows." Among instructions about overseers and deacons, 1 Timothy gives instructions about how to identify and recognize women who belong in this group (5:3-16). These instructions make it obvious that more is at stake than acknowledging that a husband has died. These widows receive financial support from the church and seem to engage in some type of ministry. Many interpreters think there was a ministerial position within the church filled by women who had lost their husbands. Just as there were elders and deacons, so there were widows. These women take a vow of celibacy as a part of their membership requirements. The author contends that young women must not be admitted to their ranks because they will want to marry and so violate their vow (5:12).

This vow may be at the root of the charge that the false teachers reject marriage (4:3). Women who were not married sometimes enjoyed more personal freedom than married women. This was particularly so if a woman did not return to the control of her father after her husband's death. Such a woman might be more free to be involved in the work of the church. In the second century, Tertullian notes how a non-Christian husband would oppose the kinds of ministries that a widow might be engaged in (*To His Wife* 2.4).

Beyond the worry that younger widows might violate their celibacy vow, 1 Timothy says that they become busybodies, saying things they should not say (5:13). This suggests that the teaching 1 Timothy opposes was promoted among the widows. This may well be why the author prohibits women from teaching in the church (2:11-15). The mention of childbirth in that proscription ties it to the command that younger widows marry and have children (5:14) rather than joining the ranks of the church's widows.

The amount of space devoted to the widows indicates that they have become an influential force within the church. This author wants to limit their numbers and their power. So he limits their membership. He insists that younger widows marry and that only older widows, those sixty and older, be admitted to the group and only if their families will not support them. These limitations intend to reduce their influence. If the author thinks that the other teaching is particularly strong among the widows (as seems likely), this is also a way to limit its spread.

First Timothy's broader response to the teaching and the widows is his bolstering of the offices of overseer/elder and deacon (3:1-13). He presents these offices as the legitimate leadership of the church. The very title of "overseer" designates such people as authorities. For 1 Timothy, an unstated but intended function of overseers and deacons is to teach and defend the faith in the face of the teaching he opposes.

Watching the Writer of 1 Timothy Work

This writer uses several strategies to convince the readers to accept his views. He cites scripture as an authority in his banning of women from teaching (2:13-15). Interestingly, he does not quote a passage but only refers to a story. Still he assumes that the reference carries weight.

More often than he cites scripture, this writer quotes church traditions (e.g., 2:5-6; 3:16; 6:15-16) that he expects the readers to recognize as correct expressions of their faith. He introduces some of these citations with the formula, "This saying is certain" (1:15; 3:1; 4:9; see similarly 3:16, "without doubt"). Often these citations do not directly support his opposition to specific teachings, but they do assure readers that he represents the beliefs that give the church its identity.

The author also turns people away from the other teaching with denigrating evaluations. He begins the letter by calling it a myth (1:4) and repeats the charge in 4:7, where it is a godless myth. In 4:7, it is also old wives' tales. He says that through prophecy the Spirit warned against the coming of such teaching (4:1). He even claims that it comes from demons. Such teaching is certainly not what anyone would want to adopt.

The most important persuasive tactic that 1 Timothy uses involves ethos, that of Paul, Timothy, and the other teachers. This letter presents Paul as the authoritative and reliable source of true teaching. The existence of a pseudonymous letter assumes that Paul is a recognized authority. The letter bolsters his authority by reminding readers that he is an apostle appointed by God and Christ (1:1). Thus, he passes on the truth to the next generation (1:18). His apostleship (and so authority) is affirmed powerfully in 2:7, where he adds his assurance of the truth of the claim. Importantly, he says this commission was to teach the truth and that it sent him to Gentiles, this letter's recipients. So God sent him to the letter's readers with the true message.

In addition, he is the prime example of the power of God to change lives and to save. He was a persecutor and the most sinful of people before he was touched by Christ. Then he received salvation through the gospel (1:12-16). Perhaps he provides the pattern for the teachers the letter opposes. Just as Paul blasphemed and was saved, so they can turn from their false beliefs and receive salvation.

The ethos of Timothy, the purported recipient of the letter, also receives significant attention. From the very beginning he is the emissary of the apostle. He is commissioned to oppose the teaching the letter rejects (1:3-7). In this role he is the faithful child of Paul (1:18; 6:12). As the church's authorized teacher, he is tasked with guarding the apostolic truth and so rejecting the other teaching (4:11-16; 6:20-21). Even having the letter addressed to him implies that he is the reliable source for correct doctrine.

Beyond the commission by Paul, Timothy is the subject of a prophecy that designated him as one who would reject false teaching (1:18-19). In addition to the prophecy, Timothy has been commissioned by the church's elders to teach and lead (4:13-14). So his authority as bearer of the true faith is broader than his authorization by Paul.

On the other hand, the ethos the writer projects for the advocates of the rejected viewpoints makes them untrustworthy. They not only lack understanding (1:6-7), they have bad consciences (1:19-20; 4:2). They renounce truth to listen to demons (4:1-2). Their rejection of Timothy's teaching demonstrates that they have a conceitedness that leads to all sorts of vice (6:3-5). Their so-called knowledge puts them out of the faith (6:21). Readers would certainly not want to associate with these kinds of teachers.

While 1 Timothy draws on many sources to persuade the readers to believe and do as the letter commands, its arguments from ethos play the largest role. If Paul and Timothy are the people described here, then the auditors should acknowledge the truth of the doctrines in the letter and shape their church's governance in the way prescribed so they can maintain that truth.

What We Learn about the Theology in 1 Timothy

First Timothy's comments about the law indicate that at least some parts of the church continue to struggle with understanding its place in the lives of Gentile believers. The author and auditors rely on the position set out earlier by Paul and his commission to Gentiles to reject the Torah observance some church members still demand. The response is less to develop a theological argument and more to rely on Paul's authority. So the church should reject the observance of certain commands because that is the position Paul takes. There is little discussion of the positive place that the law has in the church beyond the assertion that its value is to control the immoral (1:8-11).

First Timothy and Titus are distinctive in that they refer to God as savior. In 1 Timothy it is God who gives eternal life and wants all to be saved. This letter does not call Christ savior. Still, Christ is the agent through whom God's saving will is made known. The exalted Christ is also the ruler of the cosmos who will defeat all opposition to God. But it remains the saving nature of God that grounds the rejection of false teachers and the calls for ethical living. The salvation that God gives is eternal life (1:16; 6:12), but some realized eschatology is also present. Believers can begin to experience life with God now (4:8; 6:19).

While the Pastorals develop the ethos of Paul, they assume that he is an apostle and that his word is authoritative. Whereas the undisputed letters assume that apostles have authority, Paul also expects the Spirit to help the church discern God's will. In 1 Timothy (and the other Pastorals), that less-structured reliance on the Spirit has given way to the belief that a strong church structure should guard the truth that has been delivered to the church by the apostle (see 6:12). The importance of this structure is reflected in 1 Timothy's understanding of the church as the household of God (3:14-15), an institution that had a clear and rigid hierarchical structure.

The Pastorals are well known for preparing the church to exist for the long-term. They do not have the expectation of an imminent parousia. Their regulations about church offices look to preserve the church and its teachings into subsequent generations. This does not mean, however, that the Pastorals have no future aspect to their eschatology. They envision both a Second Coming and an afterlife with judgment. The pervasive concern for "godliness" in 1 Timothy is supported in part by reminding readers that it is required for them to receive salvation (4:8; 6:12-19). This letter also continues to expect the parousia (6:14-15), even viewing its own time as the "last times" (4:1-2, see the note in NRSV). Furthermore, 1 Timothy maintains the view that the incarnation, death, and resurrection of Christ initiated the eschatological era (2:5-7).

The eschatological outlook also remains shaped by apocalyptic thought. The world remains under the control of the powers of evil and Satan is at work to draw people away from God (3:7). This writer continues to look forward to the day when the exalted Christ will defeat evil and establish God's will (6:13-16).

2 Timothy

Second Timothy has so much exhortation that it has often been identified as a paraenetic letter, or as a testament of a leader who is preparing followers for life without him. The absence of a detailed description of a type of false teaching has frustrated advocates of both hypotheses. It has elements of each genre, but perhaps does not fit precisely into either. The situation this letter assumes may not require that Paul return to Asia Minor and Greece after being freed from prison. Still, the vast majority view it as pseudonymous.

Practical Problems and Responses

A central purpose of the letter is to encourage faithfulness. It urges readers to live virtuous lives that reflect their identity as believers in Christ. It seems particularly concerned to embolden believers who suffer for their faith. Paul is the example of one who endures persecution faithfully. Indeed, the author has Paul say that everyone who lives a godly life will be persecuted (3:10-12). Paul's example assures them that even if they are deserted by everyone in times of persecution, God will be with them (4:16-17). Further encouragement comes in reminders about the judgment. The faithful can trust God for vindication; the unfaithful also receive their due (1:12-13, 18; 4:1, 6-8, 14).

The lone specific teaching this letter rejects is an overrealized eschatology; some claim that the resurrection has already taken place (2:16-18). They seem to envision the resurrection as only a spiritual renewal of some sort rather than the resurrection of the dead at the judgment. There is so little attention to this matter that some interpreters think it was not a real problem but just an element of the letter's use of example to teach proper and improper Christian living. The author's only explicit response to this teaching is to note that it is false and leads people astray. He responds indirectly by referring to the coming judgment in several places (1:12-13, 18; 2:10-13; 4:1, 8, 14, 18). Giving this amount of attention to eschatology suggests that the writer was concerned about some aberrant teaching on the topic.

There are a number of places at which 2 Timothy characterizes false teaching to make it unappealing. Some of these are clearly related to the overrealized eschatology. In 2:16-19, such teaching is godless chatter and leads to impiety. Indeed, it is like gangrene. In other places the descriptions of false teachers may be more general exhortations to avoid anything that is not recognizably apostolic (3:1-9). Yet the author wants that characterization to apply to those who advocate the overrealized eschatology. Despite the derogatory characterizations of false teachers, Timothy is to correct them with gentleness and with the hope that they will repent and return to correct teaching (2:24-26). He is also to protect the church from such teaching by reminding it of proper beliefs (2:14; 4:2).

The exhortations to the younger Timothy remind him of the importance of ethical living (e.g., 2:22). At the same time, the letter connects right living and right belief (3:1-8). Even a proper handling of scripture has the goal of training people to live righteously and to do good works (3:16-17).

Watching the Writer of 2 Timothy Work

The central means 2 Timothy uses to persuade readers to follow its instructions is presenting good and bad examples; that is, ethos is central to its exhortations. It uses these exemplars to inspire readers to imitate the behavior of some and to avoid that of others. The primary good example is Paul.

The letter depicts Paul as a person who suffers for his faith and continues to trust God. He remains faithful in the midst of suffering because he relies on God's power as he looks forward to future salvation (1:8-12). Paul affirms that he is ready to die for the faith because he knows God will grant him salvation (4:6-8, 18). He also accepts these difficulties to benefit the church, to help its members, particularly Gentiles, attain eschatological salvation (2:9-10; 4:17).

Beyond implying that Paul is a figure to emulate because he is an apostle (1:1), the letter instructs Timothy (and so readers) to imitate Paul. In 1:8, Paul calls Timothy to join him in suffering (see also 2:3). Identifying Timothy as his son, Paul tells him to teach others what he has heard from Paul (2:1-2). The call for imitation is even more direct in 3:10-12. Here Paul's teaching and manner of living, including his acceptance of afflictions, are examples that set a pattern for God's people.

Paul is not the only exemplar 2 Timothy gives for his readers to emulate. A number of other people serve as examples. Timothy's mother and grandmother instilled the faith in Timothy. Onesiphorus assisted Paul and was not ashamed to be associated with him (1:16-18). Paul lists a number of people who have helped him in his ministry and circumstances in the closing paragraphs of the letter (4:9-21).

More often, this letter lists bad examples as the opposite of what readers see in Paul. While Onesiphorus has served Paul well, Phygelus and Hermogenes deserted him (1:15). Hymenaeus and Philetus are those whose teaching about the resurrection spreads like gangrene. They seem to be identified with the wicked mentioned in the quotation that follows the reference to them (2:16-19). Demas has deserted Paul because he loves the world (4:10) and Alexander did Paul harm that God will repay at judgment (4:14-15). Two characters from Second Temple period Jewish tradition also serve as examples of what not to be: Jannes and Jambres (the names given to Pharaoh's magicians) led people from the truth just as some people do in Timothy's time (3:8-9).

All of these examples, good and bad, provide patterns of living that Timothy is to adopt or to avoid. Giving examples was a common method of exhortation among moralists of the first century. When furnishing these examples, the author does not expect readers to adopt some rote imitation of the precise behavior they see in the exemplar. Instead, they supply examples of faithfulness that readers must interpret to apply to their circumstances. The author does not think believers must be in prison to imitate Paul; rather, they must be faithful in the midst of the difficulties of their lives, accepting disadvantage when faithfulness requires it.

Of course, in the letter's narrative Timothy is the direct recipient of these instructions. This might grant his successors some authority; he is to pass on Paul's teaching to reliable people (2:2). We may see here an incipient form of apostolic succession. But more generally the letter sets a pattern for church leadership. Timothy represents someone raised with faith who has been gifted by God and recognized as a leader (1:5-7). He is urged to retain correct teaching (1:13-14) and to evangelize outsiders (4:5). Importantly, he is also authorized, even commanded, to correct false teaching.

While 2 Timothy cites both scripture (2:19) and church confessions (1:10; 2:11-13), these do not directly address the problematic eschatology. They serve as assurances that the writer's views are consistent with the church's proclamation. These assurances bolster the other instructions by demonstrating that the writer's views are rooted in the core beliefs of the church.

What We Learn about the Theology in 2 Timothy

The implicit reliance on Paul's authority seen by writing in his name is supplemented by calls to "guard" or "hold" the treasure of teaching that had been passed to Timothy (1:13-14; 2:1-2). Yet this letter cites preformed traditions less often than 1 Timothy. Instead, 2 Timothy rests its teaching on the example that Paul sets. His faithfulness in the face of persecution exemplifies the way believers are to conduct themselves. Paul's suffering also mediates salvation to others (2:8-13).

As we often see in the Pauline corpus, 2 Timothy identifies God as the source of salvation, while also calling Christ savior (1:8-10). In his role as savior, Christ destroys death and brings immortality (1:10). And it is Christ in whom one believes to receive salvation (2:10-13; 3:15). Again, this salvation is primarily seen as eternal life after death (1:2, 10; 2:10; 4:8, 18).

This letter emphasizes the need to maintain a future aspect of eschatology. Not only is the overrealized eschatology explicitly rejected, the writer identifies his own time as the "last days" (3:1). These are the times when things are getting worse, as the end draws near (3:13; 4:3). The certainty of the Second Coming with judgment gives Paul assurance, provides grounds for faithfulness (1:12-13; 4:1-2), and supplies hope for those who do good (1:17-18). It also gives confidence that those who harm God's people will receive their due from God (4:14-16) and that the righteous are vindicated (1:12, 18; 4:8; 14). This letter gives more attention to the parousia than 1 Timothy and Titus. The apocalyptic mind-set in 2 Timothy retains some of the yearning for the closeness of the end.

This Pastoral Epistle focuses on giving instructions for church leadership. It sets the pattern and provides advice for how leaders should conduct their ministries. Paul as the apostle who is willing to suffer for the gospel and for his church is the central pattern of life for these leaders. He is also the source of acceptable teaching.

Titus

The letter to Titus is composed mostly of instructions about the proper exhortations that its namesake is to give to various members of the church. Older and younger men and women get instructions, as do slaves. Fewer grounds are offered for the exhortations than in other letters, but this letter also has a clearer opponent in view than was the case with 2 Timothy. Titus is also concerned to help the church think about its place within the larger world.

Practical Problems and Responses

The opponents of this letter are Jewish members of the church (the author calls them "the circumcision" in 1:10) who want the church to adhere to some unnamed elements of the Jewish purity regulations (1:13-15). They are mentioned at the beginning and the end of the letter (3:9-11) with directions to have nothing to do with them if they will not relent. So the author thinks they pose a significant threat to the church. Defeating this teaching seems to be a central goal of this letter.

The author has two major responses to this threat. The first appears at the very beginning of the letter: Titus is to appoint leaders who can teach the correct doctrines and refute the opponents (1:5-9). Establishing church offices and filling them with the right people enable the church to remain faithful to the teaching that brings salvation. Beyond the direct commissioning of elders

164

to refute false teaching, older women are directed to teach younger women the proper way to behave.

Titus's second major response to the call to take up elements of the purity laws is to define what believers should do. If they are not to listen to that teaching, the readers may wonder what they should do. This letter moves directly from rejecting the other teaching to giving instruction about how various members of the church should behave. Indeed, most of Titus is dedicated to detailing how believers should conduct their lives. Such an emphasis demonstrates that the readers do not need the teaching of the opponents.

Titus is more concerned about how outsiders view the church than what we find in the undisputed letters. In this short letter, concern about the impression that church members make on outsiders appears no less than five times (2:5, 8, 10; 3:1-2, 8; see also 2:15). Most of the virtues and behaviors the letter commends would have been approved by moralists of the day. So Titus instructs the church to live in ways that were acknowledged as the ethical standards of the day. Most interpreters think that this indicates that it comes from an era when there is less concern about the immediacy of the parousia and more thought about how to continue to live in the world as time goes on. While this seems correct, Titus also emphasizes the importance of good works (1:16; 2:14; 3:8) and maintains the contrast between existence as a believer and outsiders (2:11-13).

Watching the Writer of Titus Work

As we noted, Titus provides little support for its exhortations or its rejection of the opponents' teaching. It does cite a tradition to support its call for slaves to conduct their lives in a manner that makes belief in God attractive (2:14). It further cites a well-known line of poetry to call the opponents liars (1:12). But these do little to provide real arguments for the letter's instructions.

The dominant persuasive tool of Titus is its purported author. The greeting introduces Paul as an apostle who has been given the truth and who has been entrusted with the task of proclaiming that truth. This greeting's description of Paul's position and authority is significantly more extensive than the other Pastorals, which simply designate Paul as an apostle. Titus expects this portrait of Paul to make the letter's instructions authoritative. So again the primary kind of support for the positions taken in the Pastorals is from ethos.

Another strategy designed to turn the readers against the aberrant teaching is the letter's characterization of those who hold it. At the first mention of them, they are accused of all manner of immoral behavior, from being rebellious to being greedy and from being liars to being detestable. They are even unable to do any good (1:10-16). Then at the close of the letter the teaching is stupid and worthless and its advocates are perverted and condemned. Such a caricature intends to move the auditors to reject the other teaching because of its advocates' bad character. The contrast between them and Paul could not be more obvious. So the bad ethos of the opponents shows that their teaching should be rejected.

An indirect support for the rejection of the teaching about the purity laws may be Titus's mention of the grace through which they have received salvation (2:11-14; 3:4-7) and its identification of God as savior (1:3; 2:10; 3:4). These affirmations show that the readers do not need the opponents' teachings to be among God's saved people.

What We Learn about the Theology in Titus

Titus begins by identifying God as savior, as the one who grants eternal life (1:2-3). Unlike 1 Timothy, Titus also calls Christ savior (1:4). Both God and Christ are called savior in the greeting of this letter. Christ both redeems believers from their sins and teaches them how to live godly lives (2:11-14). So Titus may have a broader role for Christ in salvation than what we see in 1 Timothy. The broader construal of the place and work of Christ in Titus and 2 Timothy is more like what we find in the undisputed letters. The writer of Titus continues to look forward to the "hope of eternal life" (1:2; 3:7). So while the expectation about the immediacy of the parousia has diminished, the reality of it continues to be important in all three Pastoral letters.

Titus is so focused on giving instructions about church offices and proper conduct that we see little about its theology beyond what it considers to be proper Christian behavior. Still, among the issues it must address is the place of the law for Gentile believers. As it is with 1 Timothy, Titus adopts a more rigid stance toward the law than what a fuller reading of the undisputed letters suggests for Paul. Arguments about the law simply have no place in the church according to Titus (3:10-11).

Summary

Overall, the Pastorals place a great deal of emphasis on ethos as a means of persuasion. This is not surprising because they rely on Paul's authority as a primary element of the grounds of their instructions. Paul's ethos, and that of his associates and opponents, is developed most extensively in 2 Timothy, where Paul is presented as the apostle to the Gentiles who is willing to suffer for the truth of the gospel and the good of his churches. We have also seen these letters cite the church's tradition (e.g., the "faithful sayings" of 1 Timothy), and to a lesser degree scripture, as evidences for the positions they advocate. All three seem to construct less complicated theological arguments than what we see in the undisputed letters. Still they often draw implications from securely held beliefs.

The letters address different issues, with 1 Timothy and Titus opposing understandings of the way believers should relate to the law and 2 Timothy rejecting an overrealized eschatology. This may indicate that they were not written as a group or at the same time. All three do, however, call the church to conformity with the apostolic teaching as it has come through Paul and his acknowledged, even appointed, successors.

Suggested Reading

Jouette M. Bassler. *1 Timothy, 2 Timothy, Titus*. Abingdon New Testament Commentaries. Nashville: Abingdon, 1996.

Raymond F. Collins. *1 & 2 Timothy and Titus*. New Testament Library. Louisville: Westminster John Knox, 2002.

Margaret Davies. *Pastoral Epistles*. New Testament Guides. Sheffield: Sheffield Academic Press, 1996.

Lewis R. Donelson. *Colossians, Ephesians, First and Second Timothy, and Titus*. Westminster Bible Companion. Louisville: Westminster John Knox, 1996.

Mark Harding. *What Are They Saying about the Pastoral Epistles?* New York: Paulist Press, 2001.

Francis Margaret Young. *The Theology of the Pastoral Epistles*. New Testament Theology. New York: Cambridge University Press, 1994.

Chapter 15

CONCLUSION

The Apostle's Beliefs and Conversations with His Churches

O
ur survey of Paul's letters suggests that Paul was a pastoral theologian. That is, he developed and expounded the views and teachings we see in his letters in response to specific issues raised in his churches. He was constantly trying to help his churches understand how they were to live and what they should believe; not because he was a controlling personality but because he knew that what people believe influences how they live and that wholeness of life demands consistency between what people believe and how they live.

At the same time, he claims to be an apostle and thus to have authority from God. As an apostle he is given insight into the will of God that he shares with his churches. He expects them to recognize that God has authorized him to teach and to guide his churches. Yet he balances any exercise of this authority with the belief that the Spirit helps all believers discern the will of God. So he provides reasons and arguments to convince his readers to adopt the views he advocates. He is, in this sense, a genuine fellow traveler with those to whom he writes. He is exploring the contours of the life of a believer as new situations arise. He is discerning with his churches how to be faithful in a complex and often hostile setting.

It is also important for us to remember that as Paul explicates and draws inferences from the beliefs he and his churches share that he is not the original formulator of many of these teachings. He regularly quotes liturgies and confessions of the church that were not written by him, as their non-Pauline vocabulary and emphases indicate. Thus, while he is often our first evidence for a belief within the church, he is commonly not the author or originator of that belief. Still, he did draw out implications others had not seen and he used teachings in places and for purposes others had not yet utilized them. Paul accepts and relies on the formulations of the faith that were in place before he joined the church, even as he contributes to the development of beliefs within the church.

Because of the contextual nature of his writings, none of his letters, including Romans, sets out a systematic presentation of his thought that does not have particular aims in view. This means that the way he deals with particular doctrines may not represent a balanced account of his views. The differences in the ways he speaks of the law in Galatians and Romans indicate that his remarks on an important topic may respond to circumstances to such a degree that they give polemical expressions of his views that he would modify or qualify more carefully in other settings.

The contextual nature of these letters accounts for the difficulty some have in reading Paul today. He does not write missives for all churches at all times. The instructions he gives that violate what present-day readers think were never intended for all churches everywhere, but only for a particular congregation at a specific moment. As we saw in connection with his practice of receiving support from churches, what seemed appropriate to the gospel in one setting was not acceptable in another. So he accepted financial support from the Philippians, but consistently refused it from the Corinthians. His instructions, then, are conditioned by his understanding of the gospel and his perception of the church to which he writes. Thus, some of our initial impressions about his rigidity and even some ideas about his theology must be conditioned by the nature of the writings we have from him. Furthermore, churches cannot adopt Paul's advice directly. For example, a church cannot decide whether ministers should receive a salary by following Paul's directives because Paul accepts support from some people and refuses it from others. Present-day believers must find other ways to appropriate his message and guidance.

The particularity of his letters, however, can be overstated. We can identify some of his core understandings of the faith, and we turn to those as we draw this book to a close.

Everywhere it is clear that he remains a devotee of the God of Israel. All that he believes is grounded in the most fundamental claim that God is the only true god. It is this God who is known through Christ and in the experience of the church. It is also this God's will that is made known in Christ, and that revelation is consistent with the way God is known in scripture and in the experience of Israel.

At the core of his theology also stands the belief that this God had acted anew in Jesus. While this new act revealed new things or clarified some aspects of God's character, he saw it as completely consistent with how God was known in scripture (the Hebrew Bible). Paul identifies Jesus as the Messiah, the one anointed to accomplish God's will now and in the future. Paul seems to have adopted this view of Jesus from those who were in the church before him. The church had already redefined *messiah* so that Jesus, who had been executed by the Romans, could hold that position.

Paul also holds to the tradition of identifying Jesus as the "son of God." In this role Christ represents God and God's authority. Paul seems to accept that Christ was God's preexistent agent of creation, as the tradition that he cites in Philippians 2 indicates (see also 1 Cor 8:6). This identity for Jesus is confirmed by the resurrection (Rom 1:4) and sets him apart from all other messengers of God. As God's son, Christ has authority to be Lord, the one who determines how God's people are to live.

A crucial part of the identity of Jesus for Paul is that he is savior. Again, Paul was not the first to make this a defining aspect of the faith that is required to be in the church. The work of Christ, particularly his death and resurrection, brings revelation and salvation. It reveals not only that God is righteous and merciful, but also how those characteristics can both be fully engaged as God remains holy in the face of human sin while also granting relationship and forgiveness. This work of Christ is also an act of obedience to the will of God. Thus, as is always the case for Paul, Christ is subordinate to God.

Another crucial element of his theology is that the life, death, and resurrection of Jesus inaugurate the eschatological time. The resurrection of Christ is the clear signal that the end time has begun. The presence of the Spirit in the church is further clear evidence that God has begun to live among God's people as was promised for the end time. This intimate presence of God grants a foretaste of life in the full presence of God. This eschatological outlook grounds his understanding of Christ, the presence of Gentiles among the people of God, his ethical reflections, and his understanding of the church. Without this matrix through which his thought constantly interprets the world and his religious experience, his thought does not cohere. It allows him to interpret the death of Jesus, the present persecution of the church, and the dominance of the powers of evil in the present, while maintaining hope in the victory of God and the salvation of believers, which is their participation in that victory. His zeal as a missionary relies on this matrix and its hope for the future.

Paul sees the inclusion of Gentiles among the people of God as another sign that the eschatological age had dawned. The prophecies of Israel had pointed to a time when the nations would turn to Israel and Israel's God. The coming of the Spirit on Gentiles is evidence that Gentiles are now fully among the people of God. Paul's apostleship, because he is the apostle to the Gentiles, is also an eschatological phenomenon. But even as Paul is the apostle to the Gentiles, he remains committed to the priority of Israel in the gospel. As Romans 9–11 makes clear, the faithfulness of God is at stake in God's continuing commitment to Israel. God's continuing covenant with Israel is another element of continuity between God's earlier revelation and the new thing God does in Christ.

This eschatological presence of Gentiles among the people of God demanded that Paul rethink the place of the law in the community of faith. The law continues to be revelation of God and God's will, but non-Jews among the people of God must not observe its instructions, which were meant only for Jews. Rather than membership in the Mosaic covenant and Torah observance, the more central identity for all members of the church must be their faith in Christ and the relationship with other believers that faith entails. Membership within the Mosaic covenant must now be secondary to membership in the church. Paul's continuing use of scripture as authoritative revelation is shaped by the claim that Christ is the clearest revelation of God. The revelation of Christ demands a new hermeneutic, a new way of appropriating scripture for God's people. Paul's understanding of the place of the law for non-Jews is shaped by his confidence that the eschatological death and resurrection of Christ have cosmic consequences. It reconfigures the people of God so that this group includes Jews and Gentiles on equal footing. This new revelation in the gospel makes it yet more clear that God is the God of the whole world, not just of Jews. Thus, his position on the Gentile's observance of the law is grounded in his eschatology and his continuing belief in the God of Israel as the God of the entire cosmos.

Paul must help his churches interpret the delay of God's eschatological victory. While the church expected a catastrophic intervention of God to follow quickly the resurrection of Christ, Paul's letters give us a glimpse of the ways the church explained its delay. With other believers, Paul comes to emphasize the certainty of God's victory rather than its imminence. Thus he can urge his churches to remain faithful despite the unexpected delay. After all, the resurrection of Christ is the guarantee that God can overcome evil and the promise that God will defeat it and include the faithful in the victory.

This promise demands faithfulness. As much as present-day readers are accustomed to think of Paul as one who separated faith from works (or proper behavior), our reading of Paul shows that they are inseparable. The promise of salvation remained contingent on maintaining faithfulness in one's manner of life. Paul spends a great deal of his letters helping his churches understand what the proper manner of life is for believers. This demand does not mean that believers live in constant fear of condemnation, but that they recognize that their lives will be evaluated by God—even as their salvation is gained through the faithfulness of Christ. Indeed, he often refers to believers as "saints," that is, "holy ones." He can hold out such high expectations because the Spirit's indwelling enables believers to live faithfully. So even their faithfulness is an eschatological gift.

The death and resurrection of Christ serve as the central paradigm for faithfulness. As a single two-part event, it serves as the guide for the believer's life in several letters. It determines the contours of spirituality, is the pattern for apostleship and leadership provides, the exemplar for relations within the church, and reveals how valuable fellow believers are. Beyond the soteriological effects Christ's death and resurrection have, they are the exemplar for life in all its aspects. That complex of Christ's death and resurrection is the basis for the radical expectation that believers are to put the good of others ahead of their own good.

As he developed and explicated these beliefs, Paul was not simply an authority for his churches. He was an explorer, finding new ways for a broader group of people to be and live as the people of God. But even in his missionary activity he was not a loner; in his time as an independent missionary he traveled with a company of fellow missionaries. Under his leadership they established churches and proclaimed the present and coming reign of God. These communities of believers in Christ were founded on the central beliefs and claims that Paul held and shared with the wider church. Those beliefs about God, Christ, and the salvation the eschatological people of God enjoy and anticipate grounded the identity and life of these fledgling communities of believers. Following their founding, Paul became a fellow traveler with these churches. As their life circumstances raised new and difficult questions and issues, Paul worked with them to discern God's will. When issues arose about which Paul and a church disagreed, those church members stated their positions and the reasons for them. In response, Paul set out his view and tried to demonstrate how his view was more consistent with the gospel. They walked together on uncharted paths, seeking the best ways to be faithful to the will of God revealed in the Christ.

Suggested Reading

J. Christiaan Beker. *Paul the Apostle: The Triumph of God in Life and Thought.* Philadelphia: Fortress, 1980.

James D. G. Dunn. *The Theology of Paul the Apostle.* Grand Rapids: Eerdmans, 1998.

Victor Paul Furnish. *Theology and Ethics in Paul.* New Testament Library. Louisville: Westminster John Knox, 2009 (reprint of 1968 edition with a new introduction).

Richard B. Hays. *The Moral Vision of the New Testament: Community, Cross, New Creation; A Contemporary Introduction.* San Francisco: HarperSanFrancisco, 1996.

Frank J. Matera. *God's Saving Grace: A Pauline Theology.* Grand Rapids: Eerdmans, 2012.

THE LITERARY INTEGRITY OF PAULINE LETTERS

Interpreters question the literary integrity of a number of the Pauline letters. In places, it seems that multiple letters have been stitched together to form a single letter; in other places it appears that some material has been added into the original Pauline letter. This appendix discusses the most prominent of those places, giving the reasons for the question and for the positions taken throughout this book in the discussion of the various letters.

1 Thessalonians

Some interpreters question the literary integrity of 1 Thessalonians, proposing that it is a composite of two letters: 1:1–2:12 and 4:2–5:28 as one letter and 2:13–4:1 as a second. Two features support this view. First, the letter seems to have two beginnings because 2:13 sounds like the start of a second thanksgiving period. Since these usually follow the greeting in Pauline letters, it appears that an editor has simply dropped the greeting of a letter and inserted it here. This seems all the more probable because the letter also appears to have two closings. The beginning of 4:1 says, "Finally, . . ." This appears to be drawing a letter to a close, but then 1 Thessalonians goes on to several other topics. Further, if we simply drop 2:13–4:1 out, the text reads smoothly, as though nothing is missing, as we jump from 2:12 to 4:2.

The majority of interpreters, however, continue to hold that 1 Thessalonians is a single letter. The reuse of a thanksgiving formula is not unknown in the Pauline letters. A second thanksgiving also appears in Philippians (and in Colossians, which may have been penned after Paul's death). So it may be a stylistic device. Furthermore, the term translated "finally" in 4:1 is sometimes used to transition to a new topic rather than to signal the end of a writing.

Two hypotheses about interpolations raise stronger doubts about the integrity of this letter. The abrupt turn to discussion of the timing of the parousia at 5:1 has led some to identify 5:1-11 as a later insertion into the text. Rather than identifying it as an interpolation, most interpreters see it as a continuation of the immediately preceding discussion of the Second Coming (4:13-18). Some speculate that 5:1-11 is responding to a specific question raised by the Thessalonians.

The remarks about Jews in 2:15-16 pose a more substantial obstacle to maintaining the literary integrity of the letter. Many interpreters identify those verses or all of 2:13-16 as an interpolation. These verses blame the Jews for the death of Jesus, say they oppose all people, and conclude that the judgment of God has come upon them "at last." Some see a reference to the fall of the temple in the comment about the judgment of God. If that is correct, these remarks could not have been made until the year 70, over five years after Paul's death. Even if this statement does not refer to the temple, the tenor of these remarks is different from what we usually find in Paul's references to his own people. They stand in significant tension with Romans 9–11.

Despite these problems, other interpreters think Paul may have written these words. While they are uncharacteristic of his treatment of fellow Jews, Paul is quite harsh with his opponents in some places. In Philippians 3:1-3 he calls them dogs and in Galatians 5:12 he says that he hopes the people advocating the circumcision of Gentile believers will slip with the knife and mutilate their own genitals. So perhaps the 1 Thessalonian comments about judgment are not so different. In addition, readers should recognize that this condemnation is not leveled against all Jews, but only those Jews who killed Jesus and persecute the church.

The topic of 2:13-14 suggests that they belong to the flow of thought in 1 Thessalonians. These verses contribute to the letter's effort to interpret the recipients' persecution by assuring them that other believers suffer in parallel ways. The significant arguments for each view of 2:15-16 do not allow us to reach a certain conclusion. They seem to build on the important point of verses 13-14 without significantly advancing the point. So if we determine that they are an interpolation, their absence does not noticeably affect Paul's message.

The Corinthian Correspondence

Only a few interpreters continue to question the general integrity of 1 Corinthians, except for some brief interpolations. The most prominent of those is 14:33b-36. These verses call for women to be silent in the church. This instruction, of course, contradicts the instructions in chapter 11, where Paul gives instructions about how women and men should dress when they are leading worship (praying and prophesying). Beyond this problem of inconsistency with the rest of the letter, these verses appear in two different places in early copies of 1 Corinthians. In some manuscripts (e.g., Codexes D, F, and G) we find them found after verse 40, in others they appear in the position they are in our translations. Although the external evidence favors the inclusion of the verses in their present position, many interpreters think that when their dislocation in some manuscripts is combined with the internal inconsistency the evidence indicates that verses 33b (or 34) to 36 are a later interpolation. If that is the case, they originated as a comment in the margin and were subsequently misunderstood as a correction and so inserted into the text.

Most critical scholars conclude that 2 Corinthians is composed of multiple letters. A number of interpreters see 2:14–7:4 (minus 6:14–7:1, which is usually identified as an interpolation) as a letter written before the letter composed of 1:1–2:13 and 7:5-16. These parts of 2 Corinthians seem to have a different tone. While 1:1–2:13 and 7:5-16 emphasize reconciliation; 2:14–7:4 gives accounts of the conflicts, the painful visit, the tearful letter, and Titus's visit. The harsh tone of 2:14–7:4 is a contrast to the earlier sections that sound as though the conflict has been overcome. Furthermore, 7:5 resumes the account of Titus's return to Paul in Macedonia that began in 2:13 but is interrupted at 2:14. This understanding usually sees chapters 10–13 as the tearful letter mentioned in 2:1-4.

For each of these arguments in favor of finding 2:14–7:4 as a separate letter, there are significant responses. First, the sudden move away from the description of the meeting of Paul and Titus in Macedonia is understandable because the report is broken off with a doxology that begins as Paul's response to Titus's arrival. In addition, the reports of the arrival of Titus are not as similar as they seem at first. In 2:13, Paul speaks in the first person singular (I, me), while in 7:5 he speaks in the plural (we). Such a shift in the middle of the story seems unlikely. More importantly, in 2:13, Paul says that his "spirit"

(NRSV: "mind") could find no rest, while in 7:5 it is their "flesh" (NRSV: bodies) that gets no relief until Titus arrives. Finally, it is not just 1:1–2:13 and 7:5-16 that reflect a situation in which there is strife, the whole of 1–7 does. In both, for example, Paul is on the defense about his travel plans. So it seems best to see chapters 1–7 as a unity.

The differences between chapters 10–13 and the earlier parts of 2 Corinthians are more pronounced. Chapters 10–13 are quite polemical. It seems strange that Paul would turn from expressing confidence in the Corinthians in chapters 1–7, and even asking them to contribute to the collection for Jerusalem in chapters 8–9, to the biting criticisms of 10–13. Further, in chapters 1–9, Paul seems convinced that the Corinthians will reject the intruders, but in 10–13 the issue is whether they will reject them. In addition, the prospect of a visit by Paul pervades 10–13, but is nowhere apparent in chapters 1–9. Some recent interpreters have seen a rhetorical scheme that suggests that the whole of 2 Corinthians is a unity, but those observations do not seem strong enough to overcome the differences in 10–13 that we have noted.

If 10–13 is a separate letter, we must ask about the sequence of the letters. A number of interpreters identify 10–13 as the "letter of tears" (2:4), and so earlier than the other parts of 2 Corinthians. This order allows Paul to have taken care of the problem with 10-13 and to be reestablishing good relations with the Corinthians in 1–7 (8/9). Paul's remarks about the mission of Titus, however, suggest that 10–13 was written after 1–7. In 12:18, Titus has been to Corinth in the past, but in 7:14 Titus had never been to Corinth before the visit mentioned in 7:5-16. Thus, the milder letter of 1–7 did not solve the problem and Paul had to write the harsher 10–13 to try to convince the Corinthians to accept his point of view.

A number of interpreters contend that chapters 8 and 9 are also separate letters. These letters deal with the Corinthians' participation in the Collection for Jerusalem. Many find it strange that with little or no preparation Paul could turn from arguing that the Corinthians need to reject intruding teachers to abruptly asking them for money. In addition, while chapter 8 addresses the church in the city of Corinth, chapter 9 addresses the churches in all of Achaia, the region in which Corinth is located.

The last paragraphs of chapter 7 may prepare for a request as Paul rejoices in the Corinthians' repentance and in their treatment of Titus. So with good relations confirmed, Paul can ask them to help fellow believers in Jerusalem. If that is the case, chapter 9 may have been composed at the same time but perhaps distributed separately and more widely throughout Achaia. Whether these chapters were written with chapters 1–7 does little to help us understand either the chronology of events in Paul's relationship with the Corinthians or the theology of the letters as a whole. While these chapters discuss some important theological matters, they are not closely related to the subject of the rest of the Corinthian letters.

Philippians

Philippians also has characteristics that lead some interpreters to posit that it is a combination of two or three letters. The change in topic and tone at 3:2 is so jarring that some find it incompatible with the friendly and joyful mood of the rest of the letter. In 3:2–4:3 (or the paragraph may go on to 4:9), Paul tells the Philippians to watch the "dogs" who demand that Gentiles be circumcised. He then compares the blessings he has as a believer in Christ with what he had before. The section also includes a reference to "enemies of the cross" (3:18-19). No other parts of Philippians address opponents within the church.

The other suggested letter is 4:10-20. It is here that Paul finally thanks the Philippians for the gift of financial support they had recently sent. Since it seems strange that he waits until the end of the letter to thank them, some see this thank-you as a separate letter.

The majority of interpreters, however, continue to see Philippians as a unity. The sudden remarks about the "dogs" may well fit the kind of argument Paul makes throughout the letter. From its beginning, Paul points to examples the Philippians should imitate as guides for their conduct. He has already given Christ, himself, Timothy, and Epaphroditus as examples to imitate. Ancient writers and speakers often gave examples to help people see how they should live. They also gave bad examples to clarify how their audience should not live. The "dogs" of 3:2 may well be a case of citing a bad example. If so, they may not have been present or even a threat to the Philippian congregation. Similarly, the "enemies of the cross" may refer to those who persecute the church. Such opposition had already been mentioned in 1:28. The specter of these bad characters serves as the foil against which to emphasize the good characteristics of the other examples. So rather than being evidence of the insertion of a separate letter, they may play an important role in the letter's argument.

The thanks for the gift may come where it does to conform to conventions of giving and expectations of reciprocity that were familiar to Paul and the Philippians, but not to us. There were clearly set ways that such relationships were to function in the ancient world. Yet Paul often redefined such relationships. Perhaps waiting to thank the Philippians until the end both follows some conventional expectations and helps redefine what their gift means. In any case, the seemingly strange placement of this section alone is not enough to place in doubt the letter's literary integrity.

INDEX

Abraham, 94–95, 97, 98, 100, 106, 110, 130

affliction, 52, 55, 85, 134, 139, 140, 162. *See also* suffering

afflictions of Christ, 134
    of Paul and apostles, 52, 85, 162

afterlife, 25, 53, 54, 69, 160. *See also* resurrection

agent (Christ as), 133, 152, 159
of creation, 133, 136, 171
of the end time, 6, 122

Alexander the Great, 12–13, 22, 23n2

Antioch/Antioch church, 4, 41, 50, 92, 99

anti-Semitism, 3, 43, 44

apocalyptic, 37, 54, 55, 58, 129, 143, 160, 164

Apollonius, 21

Apollos, 62, 71

apostle/apostleship, 35, 52, 56, 61, 77–88, 92–94, 98, 104, 105, 107, 111–12, 124, 130, 142, 144, 145, 147, 149, 152, 158, 160, 162, 164, 165, 167, 169, 172, 173

apostolic authority, 4, 81, 125, 142, 144, 149, 163

apostolic teaching, 142, 143, 158, 161, 167

Apuleius, 25

asceticism, 17, 20, 21, 132

ataktoi, 141

atonement, 73

baptism, 5, 26, 97, 98, 100, 107, 108, 131, 132, 134, 135, 136, 137, 147

Barnabas, 41, 50, 93

body, 77, 94, 178
    as metaphor for church, 67–70, 108

Cephas. *See* Peter

character. *See* ethos

Cicero, 25, 35, 129

circumcision, 41, 42, 91, 92, 95, 97–100, 104, 106, 109, 110, 116, 119, 134, 146, 164, 176, 179

collection for Jerusalem, 78, 79, 81, 103, 104, 178

common good (good of the church), 119, 120, 122, 134, 149, 167, 173

confession, confessional material, 4, 150, 163, 170

covenant, 7, 38, 40–44, 96, 97, 99, 100, 106, 107, 108, 132, 134, 147, 150, 172
    new covenant, 5, 16, 42, 43, 85, 99, 134, 136, 146

creation, new. *See* new creation

cross/crucifixion (execution), 5, 6, 9, 39, 63, 64, 66, 72, 73, 74, 75, 78, 79, 84, 94, 111, 119, 121, 122, 155, 171, 179

curse, 68, 93, 94

cynics, 17–29

Day of the Lord, 56, 140–41, 143. *See also* parousia

deacon, 40, 78, 156, 157

death, 12, 14, 16, 24, 26, 40, 58, 74, 79,